Praise 1

"'Wild Joy' is a must-re ......s you on an intimate and honest journey of her struggles and victories. She reveals how she discovered wild joy, despite the painful circumstances of life. She shares how you too can not only have the peace that passes understanding but the abundant life of wild joy that we are promised by our faithful God."

—**Heidi Frederick**
Author of Faith, Hope and Love, but the
Greatest of These is Love

"Joannie understands joy because she has walked through the pain, discouragement, and despair needed to embrace the abundance that God promises for our lives. She knows that to live and to live fully, we must accept the joy that often comes in the very middle of our heartaches. She lives each day embracing love, healing, and peace. In 'Wild Joy,' she openly shares her examples with others so they can also embrace the joy that brings freedom and treasures (2 Corinthians 5:20)."

—**Ree Clark**

Beautiful Warrior and mom of three adult children

"'Wild Joy' is a must-read. You can feel the heartbeat of each journey brought forth in this book. Author Joannie Garner's intimate story draws you closer to God and challenges you to persevere and go higher in God. She teaches you to enjoy the adventures of life as you walk closely with God. The transparency of Author Joannie Garner's life's journey shared in this book will bring forth tears, laughter, courage, strength, and healing to families and healing in relationships. You will certainly learn to find wild joy in the simple things in life despite the hardships you may endure."

—**Dinah Cook**
CEO of Changing Your World Coaching Intl LLC
Author of Fixing A Broken Glass **and speaker**

"Joannie states the goal of this book is 'how to find joy and discover your own.' Meeting her at seventy-four has been an uplifting experience and encouraged me; I feel like I have been infused with something I didn't know I needed. Joannie has set aside grieving and accepted the wonderful gifts of our good God. We all can learn so much from her, especially how to recognize our struggles with God. She states I had to be willing to do things I have never done in order to have the things I have never had. That is true for all of us."

—Gail Box Ingram

**Poet and author of Komerebi: Light Shining Through,
The Old Basketball: A Story of Compassion**

WILD JOY

Moments Captured in the Wild, Weird and Wonderful Spaces of Everyday and Extraordinary Life.

BY JOANNIE P. GARNER

Wild Joy
Trilogy Christian Publishers A Wholly Owned Subsidiary of Trinity Broadcasting Network

2442 Michelle Drive Tustin, CA 92780

Cover design by: __

For information about special discounts for bulk purchases, please contact Trilogy Christian Publishing.

Manufactured in the United States of America

10 9 8 7 6 5 4 3 2 1

Library of Congress Cataloging-in-Publication Data is available.

ISBN: 978-1-63769-656-9

E-ISBN: 978-1-63769-657-6

This book is dedicated to my parents, who God used to bring me into this world. They

were not here to witness the publishing and read Wild Joy, but I know they are looking down

from heaven smiling at what the Lord has done in my life.

Acknowledgments

To my Beautiful Warrior sisterhood, there is no one like you. You challenge me, cheer me on, and give me purpose. We are better together.

To my amazing children, Seth and Josie, I can't imagine living life without being your

mom. I have found the wildest joys in partnering with Jesus in parenting you. I will always love

you. I feel like the richest woman in the world watching you grow into who God made you.

To my handsome, selfless, big-hearted husband, Tim. God gave me the best when He gave you to me. I am honored to be your wife, and I would say, "I do," again and again. I love you. You know, I married you so I could kiss you anytime.

To my family: my sisters, brother, aunts, uncles, nieces, nephews, cousins, grandmothers, mother-in-law, I thank you for showing me acceptance and what not giving up looks like.

To my friends who are like family, I appreciate your friendship and love.

Ree, my sunshiny friend, your honest feedback helped me to write with more of an open heart. I am grateful for your kindness and support.

Dinah, my sweet author friend who agreed to read and review *Wild Joy* in less than two weeks. I am thankful for your "Yes" and eagle eye.

Jill, my dance-loving Jesus friend, I am humbled by your encouraging words and daily example of carrying your cross.

Heidi, my compassionate friend who listened to my endless insecurities and excuses. Thank you for guiding me towards the finish line. All our conversations were lifesavers!

Gail—a spiritual mother who freely shares her wisdom.

To my Prayer Warriors, you know who you are, and I couldn't have completed this book without your faithfulness to pray. I am humbled by your commitment.

To you, my joy-seeking readers, I finished it for you! I see you!

To King Jesus, it is all for your glory!

You did it: you changed wild lament into whirling dance; You ripped off my black mourning band and decked me with wild-flowers. I'm about to burst with song; I can't keep quiet about you. God, my God, I can't thank you enough.

Psalm 30:11-12 (MSG)

CONTENTS

Foreword

But we have this treasure in jars of clay to show that this all-surpassing power is from God and not from us.

2 Corinthians 4:7 (NIV)

"It is no accident that you are holding this treasure of a book in your hands. I'm humbled and honored to have the author of this book as a true close friend. Her story could have so many optional endings and scenarios, but this girl fought and continues to fight to be the Joannie that Almighty God is creating her to be. That is the treasure!

"Joannie has chosen to face the trials and spiritual warfare in her life head-on! The things the enemy meant to break her have only made her faith stronger. She's real, and she's raw. She's transparent, and she is not afraid to tell you what she is feeling, thinking, or experiencing. The world needs more women like Joannie. Women who are authentic in their faith and pursue the abundant, adventurous, wild, and joyful life that God has planned for every single one of us. We just have to choose to cannonball into the depths of His love and experience the life He has in store for those of us who pursue Him instead of being swayed by the momentary things the world has to offer!

"In true Joannie fashion, please run yourself a tub of hot water and soak in the stories she has poured her beautiful heart and soul into. When the water gets cold, put on your most favorite pajamas and read some more. I promise you won't want to put this book down!

"Ponder the lessons lived and learned, and ask the Lord to please help you see life through eyes like the wonderful, hip, Jesus-chasing girl that Joannie is. Joannie is that friend that will continually point to Christ in all things! I promise you'll want the zest for a life lived well for God's kingdom like my friend who is about to become your friend too!"

—Jill Wells
Beautiful Warrior
Dance Studio Owner, Leap of Faith

Preface

I wrote *Wild Joy* because I knew I had to get my message out that you can live in a space

of grief and joy. I lost my mom at a young age in 1986 and didn't know how to allow myself to feel the sadness. I was only twelve and the oldest of three other siblings. The year 2021 presented many opportunities to heal from her loss. I found that you need to feel, deal, and heal. Many people don't know how to feel their emotions. I was once like that and discovered much sorrow in the grief but also overflowing joy in the celebrations of life. I learned how to share space with deep sorrow and wild joy.

Much of the discovery came from one of the greatest losses, my dad. He died

Unexpectedly, 2019 in his sixties. No one saw it coming! It felt like a horrible nightmare I couldn't wake up from. My dad was a troubled man and died with much sorrow, but he was a happy man and had a bigger-than-life personality. He and my mom never discovered their purpose. The best gift and thank you I can offer them is to live in my purpose.

I pray as you read my stories, you allow yourself to laugh, cry, scream, jump, shout, dance, sing, hope, and forgive. My prayer is you learn to love again, not just others but yourself,

and you open your heart to love God. As your heart opens again, so will your life. As you open your life up again, you will find unexpected gifts, surprises, and God winks. Life is full of laughter and sadness. When you embrace those moments every day, you find not only the ordinary but extraordinary experiences of life.

I lived to tell the stories, and so will you! It takes a desire to fight and stay present. With

the help of God, anything is possible. To forgive my mom and dad, to allow love to take place

13

of anger, hurt, and abandonment is one of those "but God…" moments. One way I learned to

express my emotions is through poetry. I hope you enjoy them.

Only One Mom

Parts of you, Mom, are parts of me.

No words to explain what you mean to me.

Only one you, only one me.

Life took you away from me way too early.

I was only twelve and too young to understand your pain.

You were only thirty and too young to understand your own pain.

One day we will be reunited again.

Until then, I will hold on to memories.

Thank you for bringing me into this world,

You showed me I am worth fighting for.

What you couldn't do on this earth, I will accomplish.

I will never know why you had to leave so early.

One day, another time, I'll hold your hand, and you'll hold mine.

We will embrace and never be apart again.

I have this hope to be anchored in.

I'll love you til eternity.

Joannie Garner, 2019

My Dad Disappeared

I am mad,

I am sad.

My dad is gone.

Is this a bad dream?

Is this my reality?

My dad is gone.

One day here, the next disappeared.

The shock has faded a bit,

But denial is knocking on my heart.

I want to wake up from this bad dream.

I want to know this isn't real.

My dad can't really be gone.

Too young, too many dreams left to die.

An exhale, a deep sigh.

My dad went to his eternal home.

Joannie Garner *(day 56 of his death)*

Intro into Wild Joy

Now I'm jumping for joy, and shouting and singing my thanks to him.

Psalm 28:7 (MSG)

This is what I know. I have spent a lifetime looking, seeking, searching for something. Something more.

What I found was joy. Who knew all the searching would lead me to an untamed and intangible gift I call wild joy.

The years of experiencing stuffed and boxed emotions left me empty and full of questions. I decided to do something about all of those questions. I went on a search for answers.

There are still many answers to be found, but what I found, I wanted to share with all of you.

Wild joy is what this book is about. A joy that can't be bought or fabricated.

I found that God's love is a lot like wild joy, it can't be contained in a box, and it can't be harnessed or tamed.

My belief is you haven't lived until you have discovered real joy, the wild joy, skip a beat in your heart because you felt something new.

My story is just one. A story, a bit of an experiment. How long can one go without joy? To live without the rainbow that comes after the rain is not truly living.

My prayer is that my joy stories will stir your own.

I lived most of my life without joy. In the past decade, my greatest discovery has been in finding something stronger and more solid than happiness. In the sorrow, in the sadness, in the darkness, and the pain is where I found wild joy.

The greatest surprise is you can live in a space of loss, sadness, grief, and love, peace, and joy at the same time. I think many people feel bad about grieving and then never really embrace it, which holds them back from the truest expressions of themselves, the wild joy that Jesus paid a high price for you to experience.

When joy is found within, it is a rare commodity, a precious jewel. My life has forever been changed. I can't wait for you to find your own precious jewel.

This is not a book about how to or steps one, two, three. You will be disappointed if you are looking for a cookie-cutter solution. Joy can only be found on a journey with Jesus.

I spent many days thinking joy was found in happiness. This mindset will not only leaves you empty but also confused. Have you ever asked yourself, why do bad things happen to good people? I will explore that because it has been a question looming in my mind.

Questions without answers can cause you to turn away from your faith. My book is a call towards your faith. A call to your creator who thinks you were worth dying for.

Loss, hurt, pain, and disappointment can leave you with many lingering questions. Joy will not only awaken something dormant in your soul but also evoke emotions in your heart you haven't felt in a very long time.

To swim in grief and pain. To navigate joy and love. To feel grief and joy is to live.

I want to introduce you not only to some of my happy moments but also to a lifestyle of happiness—a deeper call to happiness. Do not confuse this with a perfect, happy life that is void of pain and heartache but a celebration, a lifetime of pure bliss.

Life is still full of loss and pain. Our hearts will still hurt beyond human understanding. Our minds will still, at times, feel like they might explode. Our bodies may not experience full healing until we meet our creator. But God…

Joy is truly found in those moments of not being okay. When you accept not being okay with the way your life turned out, then you are closer to finding joy.

I have struggled with the idea, the theory of contentment. What does content even mean? I found my own definition. To be okay with where my life is, to still be okay when life changes because it will, to be okay when things or people stay the same as you change, and to still want "more."

I am so happy for you if joy is a fruit you are familiar with. If you were playing the warm, hot, and cold game, where would joy fit in? Are you freezing cold and feeling so far away, or are you burning up and so close you can taste joy on your lips? When you accept the things you cannot change and stop trying to fix the things you can't, you are closer to joy.

Do you want to go on a treasure hunt? A hunt to find the riches of life, not just in material possessions but in those intangible gifts, the fruit Jesus created, the fruit of the spirit.

Do you remember as a young child catching lightning bugs? What did you do with them? You put them in a jar to keep them forever. Then you returned a few days later to see they had died or somehow escaped.

Joy can feel like that, one day to be caught and the next day to die or fly away.

You can't fully understand joy unless you have fully experienced sorrow. To love deeply is to grieve deeply. To see loss is to see joy.

I know pain all too well and will share my painful experiences. My prayer is as you sort through your own life, you will see glimpses of joy. As you embrace and stop resisting, you will live in the everyday and extraordinary moments.

"God! God! I am running to you for dear life; the chase is wild" (Psalm 7:1, MSG).

Keep running after God.

Keep moving forward.

Keep seeking, keep searching.

Keep going after the *more*.

You will eventually find it! You can't outrun your pain. You can't outrun God!

Keep running, one step forward at a time.

Joy is one of the best gifts that is absolutely free! Oh, it might cost you something, your pride, your anger, your unforgiveness. A question to ask yourself, are you willing to pay the price? Jesus paid a big price for you.

I hope you never stop capturing those moments when joy shines the brightest. I hope as you read my words, your heart opens more and more to experience those joyful times.

Most people do not even leave home without their phones. This means that you are always armed with a camera. Your cameras can be used to capture moments of joy.

You don't want those moments. They can be quickly gone! Nature draws me in, and I want to capture it all. How many times do we snap a picture and think, *This does not even come close to what I am seeing?*

I am a nature girl and drawn to God's beauty. A sunrise, sunset, flower, butterfly, trees, or mud puddle. I try to stop and remember that without God, we are left without beauty. He is the creator of all beautiful things. Beauty can't always be captured on a camera. Have you tried to snap a pic and thought, *No way, this doesn't do it any justice?* I compare beauty to joy. They both have to be first felt. You can capture the beauty of life in your thoughts and in your hearts. I hope you will see more of the beauty in your own life as you read this book. As you see the beauty, I hope joy is unraveled.

CHAPTER 1:
My Why

God deals out joy in the present, the now. It's useless to brood over how long we might live.

Ecclesiastes 5:20 (MSG)

I made it! We did it! You, my beautiful reader, helped me finish this book! Thank you! When I didn't know if I could come up with one more word, I saw your face. I pictured your life and your struggles, cause, let's face it, we all have them!

Feeling tired and weary can leave you with a restless soul. I could see the smile on your face as you read my words. I could hear your fears, see your tears and feel your pain. I don't know the details of your pain, but I have lived my own pain. We have that in common, my joy-seeking reader. I do hope we will cultivate a friendship as you turn the pages of this book.

I knew that I had to finish this project to show you what is possible. If I can do it, so can you! My prayer is you will find your own possibilities and path. A path that leads to wild joy.

I discovered writing a book is similar to all the things of life, like lessons we have to learn the hard way. You will make many mistakes, like millions of them, as you go throughout your everyday. Some of your days will be ordinary and feel mundane and leave you wanting more. Those days might even leave you feeling worn out and wondering what the point of living is!

You don't even want to get out of bed to take the dog out to potty. Going to work might feel like a struggle too. The everyday duties and responsibilities start weighing you down. My weight might look different than your weight, but we all have weight that makes our load feel unbearable.

You might find happiness in caring for your family. Those mundane tasks could be joy sparkers. You could be married to a spouse who cooks fabulous meals, doesn't mind loading the dishwasher or taking the dog out. I can only dream a little about where your life has found you reading my pages. You might be single and order take-out, which means no cooking and no cleaning! Your life and everyday tasks are going to be different than mine.

But maybe you are just tired, no matter where you find yourself. You are tired of doing the same thing day after day and seeing no change. Not feeling any internal changes, you keep hoping to wake up feeling different, but wake up the same. Change is on the way!

Who knew small, simple things really mattered?

You are capable and deserving of change.

You could be living in those extraordinary days and not even know it!

I am here to help you see it all, the good and the bad, to include the ugly.

Those mistakes you made don't define you. You are defined by something much greater. You get to decide if you are going to learn lessons or repeat patterns. I'll be sharing my own lessons. In all the moments, I found the wild, weird, and wonderful spaces. I pray you will find them too and more.

God will allow you do it alone and create your own roads. And believe me, I created my own yellow brick road. I did not find the wizard. I was left encountering the wicked monkeys. Thankfully God wasn't too far behind. Actually, He was upfront waiting for me.

ATTRIBUTES OF GOD

When you know the true attributes of God, you realize that God and man are not the same. God was perfect, and you are not. I know, I know. Why did I have to be the one to tell you. He knows all things, and you do not. Again, so sorry to tell you, but someone had to. LOL.

The days of traveling my yellow brick road, God allowed me to do life my own way. He let me skip, fall, and struggle. He is not a tyrant and doesn't force His ways on you.

He will allow you the beautiful space and freedom to discover life. He will also allow opportunities for you to experience the life Jesus died for you to live.

You might have grown up in church and have a distorted view of God. You see Him as someone who is mean and ready to smite you. I don't know your view of God, but I want to introduce you to my view of God as the loving Father I trust. He doesn't wait for you to mess up so He can punish you. When you mess up, He offers you, His grace.

I am curious where you find yourself right now. Do you smile when you think about God, or do you frown? If I could see your facial expression, I would know a bit more about your view of God. I could see what the word God evokes in you.

I have found God as a heavenly Father who is always guiding me, leading me, and trying to show me His way. He will let you pursue your heart's desires even if it brings harm because He gives us free will.

Isn't it funny when you do find yourselves in a mess, God gets the blame? You become mad at God and close your heart off to him. Don't you think He might know a thing or two about our hearts? After all, isn't God the one who formed us from His image?

He knows us the best. Our heart may lead us astray, but God says, He will never leave you nor forsake, and I believe Him! I don't know what your story consists of. You could write your own book on all the heartache you survived. I have my pom-poms in hand cheering you on; write the book. Write that book! Don't wait until you are almost fifty like me. Do it *now*! I have taught my kids, the best time to do anything is *now*.

Most of this book was written in those painful times. My perfectionism tendencies kept me from publishing it sooner. All of that stinking thinking! Why would someone want to read my book? What do I have to say that hasn't already been said? I can blame some of those negative thoughts for being the oldest. So don't blame me; it is birth order issues. Ha! Can I get a raise of hands for all of my firstborns? Thank you.

We oldest have to stick together. I see you, middle children, too. I have watched you grow up and wonder where you fit in with your family. I am married to you, babies. My husband is the youngest of three boys. One of the things I love the most about him is his sense of humor. All you last born, thank you for keeping us laughing. Thank you for helping me not to take myself so durn seriously.

If you are looking for life to slow down, then keep on looking. You are going to have to be the one who learns how to park your car and get out to enjoy the view. I know God is speaking to you. He spoke to you when you purchased this book. You are so loved!

A quiet place can be hard to find. I had to sit in my car to hear my own thoughts. You might be living the opposite and have to leave your home because it is too quiet. A dear loved one might have passed, and you are in a season of loneliness. I am so sorry for your loss. Loss I know all too well.

GOT PEACE

Loss, loss, and more loss; in my searching for something more, I found peace. It seemed I was always trying to find peace. I think I was looking for a cheap peace, the peace the world had to offer. I tried that peace, and it wasn't for me.

I wanted God's peace! A peace within that would settle my soul. I also needed a bit of quiet, not just in my mind but in my home. That won't always be my story when I am an empty nester. As I was putting the finishing touches on *Wild Joy,* I craved peace more than ever! I wanted to hear my thoughts. I wanted to read my words out loud. I wanted to experience the peace of Christ.

When you do find peace, it is a fight to keep it. Situations and people will try to steal your peace. I lost my peace man times but always found myself searching for it again.

When I did find those quiet times, God would reveal the motives in my heart. He would show me my desires. He would remind me of the dreams that I only talked to Him about. Do you have desires or dormant dreams? What are they? Take the time to write them down. Talk to a trusted friend about them. Speak them out and give them words. Declare them!

You only get one chance in life.

In those quiet times, the why questions came up. Why did I want to finish this book? Why was it important for me to get my stories out for you to read? Why did I struggle with finishing this project? There are so many whys swirling around waiting to be acknowledged and answered. As busyness fools the world, are you taking the time to discover why questions?

The Lord revealed the "more"! You, my precious reader, *you* were the "more"! I had to dig deep, ask the hard questions, do I really have something of value to offer you.

I wanted to be sensitive to those I care about. It was a balancing act to share my story and honor. You will notice, I only shared names of my immediate family. I wanted to honor the privacy of my friends and family. You can also fill in the blank with your friends when I am sharing stories.

The whole process of writing and editing, I keep hearing this, the truth liberates you to fly, to be free! Let's go after that freedom. Moving forward one step, one word at a time.

GOT LEGACY

When I got stuck, I saw the sweet angelic faces of my grand-babies. The ones I would meet and the ones who I would never get to meet on earth. I joke with my teens about having four to six children each. I mean, that would make up for my husband and me only having two children, right! This was so much bigger than you and bigger than me. This was about legacy! Who would carry on my legacy? I knew that my journey to joy was not to keep to myself. I saw the *why* in praying for you. Asking the Lord what He wanted me to say and how He wanted me to say it, to release it with words in this book.

This book is my words to you, my offering, my surrendering, my laying it all down for you. My gift wrapped up in a red bow offered in a book format. I pray you know how much God

loves you just the way you are but way too much to leave you there. I pray my words

evoke a sense of wonder and activate that childlike faith within you. Maybe you don't even know what childlike means; it means just like it sounds. To be childlike.

When you get stuck, start asking those hard questions. It might not be *why*! It might be *who*! Who do you believe? What greater power do you believe in? I believe in Jesus Christ as my savior. If it was all about me and my limited, small thinking, then I would have given up. Not just in my book but in life.

I have asked myself many times in those deep dark places only I know about. What is the point of waking up and facing another tomorrow? Why go through this pain to face another day of loss, disappointment, and heartache? I found the whys of life, and I pray you will too! I found healing, wholeness, and freedom in God's Word. You will see many verses that are

meaningful to me, I hope they bring refreshment to your life.

"Lord, you know all my desires and deepest longings. My tears are liquid words, and you can't read them all" (Psalm 38:9, TPT).

The verse above speaks so much to my heart; I feel known in my pain, I feel seen in my tears, I feel accepted in my heartache. Most of all, I feel loved! To feel loved! Do you feel loved? What does it mean to not live a life of feeling loved? What does it mean to let your pain and hurts over rule God's love? I have watched friends turn their back on God. They have rejected the love that once held them in security.

They somehow stopped believing in God's love. They no longer believed that God loved them. They also questioned their source of power. They no longer knew if God was their source. I know from experience; my power is limited and runs out.

In 2020, during the covid, I had a friend stop by. We hadn't seen each other in a year. All of the unknown with covid, people just didn't get out and visit each other.

I could quickly tell, in our conversation, she was hurting but tried to act like she was okay. I knew better, and you know when something is bothering your friend. I could tell life had beat her down. I didn't know how bad until she said there were many gods, and the Bible is just stories. She no longer believed in who I know God to be. She no longer believed the way she used to believe.

I saw her passion for life diminish. I knew she was struggling but had no clue how bad. Her sense of wonder, the childlike to believe, was no longer there. I didn't know what to do or say in the conversation. I didn't want to be disrespectful, but I also didn't want to listen one more minute to what she was saying about the Jesus I loved!

I gave her a hug, and she got in her truck. We departed agreeing to disagree, and I thought many times about if she was okay. Of course, I am praying for her. I hope she is reminded of God's mercy, love, and grace. I hope she opens her heart up once again to Jesus

We were friends for several years. We attended events and church together. She was a Beautiful Warrior I watched grow. She knew my door was always open to her. The day we parted, I honestly didn't know if we would ever see each other again.

I pray she does awaken to the truth and her eyes and ears are open again to God's unconditional love. I didn't understand her beliefs. I knew that her pain caused a tug of war in her heart and mind. I can understand feeling hurt when bad things happen to good people. When it seems life only takes from you.

I am so sorry if this is how you feel or have felt in the past. Sometimes, people don't do a great job of exemplifying Christ. I hope my words will renew hope and bring life to your confused places. I know God can heal those deep wounds. He did it for me, and He will do it for you!

To live is to die; to die is to live.

He is patiently waiting for you to ask. A child asks a lot of questions, and the Lord is calling you back to the childlike faith. I pray you will experience childlike faith and a sense of adventure as you embark on this new season. There is this whole new world waiting to be discovered by you! In your asking, you find answers. In your searching and seeking, you find the one who created you.

"You will seek me and find me when you seek me with all your heart" (Jeremiah 29:13, NIV).

What are you going to do when you meet the real you? The real you without any pretense. The masks come flying off. There is no one to perform for, pretend to and please; there is only an open space for you to find you, the real you. The you Jesus died for. My audience is, for one, Jesus. I do it for the one. Jesus died for the one lost sheep; that might be you! Jesus is your great shepherd.

There is a knowing that Jesus was and is and will always be the answer. At least the answer for me. God is the one who created life and life so beautifully. I want to introduce you to my creator. The one who wants to kiss your booboos away. His love will heal those deep wounds. Just like my friend, it is okay if you don't believe the way I do. I am still cheering you on. I am still believing you will ask all the right questions. Don't leave out the why questions. I hope you discover more than you could have imagined as you ask *why*.

CHAPTER 2:
Got God-fidence

Confidence: feeling or showing confidence in oneself.

God-fidence: living out confidence in Christ, not confident in self.

Writing started for me when I was eleven years old. I made up my own poem. I wish I had a copy of it to share with you. I can tell you my words rhymed and more than likely consisted of cheesy content. This poem did not have very friendly content. You could say the words were colorful. My colorful back in the 80s was much different than what kids are speaking, singing, and writing these days.

This memory of the poem was so special; I honestly don't have many memories of my mom. The ones I do have, I cherish in my heart and don't want to forget, but I have not always felt that way. It took years of healing my broken heart.

In 1986, I was at a friend's house, and I got a phone call from my mom asking me to come home. She found something I wrote and was not entertained by it. I sure wasn't thinking about the poem I wrote. Who leaves their colorful poem on the table for their parents to see! I guess I did! It was accidentally left behind by my young tween self.

The last thing I wanted was for my mom to find the poem. I honestly don't remember much about that day except she held me responsible.

As I look back, I can see maybe my mom did care about me. Maybe, I did matter! What I did mattered; my life actually mattered. My mom found my writing and read it. She took an interest in my life. She was home, and she found the poem. She took the time to call me out and hold me accountable for my behavior.

I also won't ever forget the time she got mad at me and spanked me with a paint stirrer. I am not sure what I did; it probably had to do with my sassy mouth. You know those small, thin boards? Well, I was an active child and always on the go. This spanking was no different. I was hopping all around, telling her to stop. She got me really good on my thigh. When I saw the mark she made, I was mad! I was thinking, *how dare she!* Who did she think she was leaving a welt on my leg? That is my naïve twelve-year-old self-talking. Oh my...

I witnessed a lot of abuse but can honestly say my mom wasn't physically abusive to me or my siblings. I am grateful for God's protection. I am sad for the times I witnessed abuse she suffered. A small girl does not want to ever see her mom being smacked or punched. The little girl inside of me felt helpless. Can anyone relate?

I am sad for me but much sadder for the abuse my mom suffered in the short thirty years she was alive. She watched her dad beat her mom. She also saw her dad physically abuse her brother. She more than likely saw other abuse. I never got to have conversations about abuse with her. I never really got to have any conversations with her.

I never actually saw her being slapped around by her boyfriends. I only saw the bruises and the sadness in her eyes. I can see she tried to protect me from the abuse.

It's now hard not to see a pattern of abuse in my family. I am sad to share, my mom's family were not the only ones who dealt with abuse. Unfortunately, my dad's family was also torn apart by abuse. Sadly, both of my grandfathers were alcoholics. My dad's father didn't stick around long, at least not long enough to take care of his family.

My dad was the oldest son, and I am sure he carried so much responsibility; he thought he needed to take care of everyone. I get it; I have been there! He carried the heavy weight of his family. This began a journey of drugs? I am sure it started small, smoking pot. A life of relying on something, anything to numb began for him. He experienced great loss when his brother, who was only seventeen years old, died. I know this was a great tragedy for their family. How does one cope with all the pain?

All of this pain and abuse, what does one do with it? I didn't even get into all the different types of abuse. I am sorry if you ever experienced abuse, especially at the hands of your parents are ones who were supposed to protect you. People just didn't talk about abuse back then and still don't! You more than likely know someone who is being abused. Abuse is not a respecter of persons; it happens everywhere! Many are being abused right now and stay silent. They stay silent because of the shame.

I know the way my parents were raised made me want to be a better parent. I did not want to repeat the same patterns. I surely didn't want to be abusive to my children. I wanted to be a present parent. I wanted to be a parent who loved them. Jesus knows a thing or two about abuse; He endured abuse and death.

Back to the story where my mom left a welt on my leg. I told my mom, "Wait until I see Grandma. I am telling her what you did to me!" Of course, by the time we went to visit my

grandmother, the welt was gone. I chuckled, thinking about this, because what was my grandma

going to do? I guess I thought she was going to have a talk with my mom. That even sounds

strange sharing because of the abuse that happened in both of their lives.

My mom correcting my behavior was a time I felt loved by her. She was correcting my behavior and loved me enough to not let me get away with whatever I did. I more than like was being a bit sassy, and I wonder where my daughter gets it! Hmmm...

I felt loved by my mom, even with the welts on my legs. It might seem strange for some to hear. Or you might be thinking, *I get it!* If you aren't relating to my story, then I am sure you have your own story of loss or abuse. We all have a story.

PARENTING AIN'T EASY

As the world tries to tell you how to raise your children, just know you are doing a great job! Tell another parent they are doing a great job too! We parents need to stick together.

When my children were young, I had no problem spanking them. My husband wasn't one to spank. My kids didn't hear the famous saying, "Wait until your dad gets home." When Dad got home, I already handled business, and we had a chill night. My kids knew I was not one to play with. I would correct their behavior and give them a choice, and most of the time, they picked the three licks. I wanted them to pick the grounded or the sentences. The teacher in me loved when they had to write sentences.

Now, if you are angry, I don't recommend you spank. Your children don't deserve you taking your anger out on them. Along with sentences, I liked to give my children the choice to pick out a Bible verse that applied to their onery behavior. If it was Josie, all the verses had to do with the mouth and heart.

That sassiness had her drinking apple cider vinegar too. I think she actually started liking it. She wasn't going to let me know it bothered her. Now, my son, he acted like he couldn't breathe when he had to drink it. That kid had the worst gag reflux!

There are many ways to correct behavior. Some spank, some don't, some offer time-outs, some give sentences, the lesson is you get to pick. You get to parent in a way that works for your child and your family. My goal was to make sure my children knew consequences were a thing. I knew part of my job as a mom was to prepare them for the real world.

The story I shared about my mom finding the colorful poem was very pivotal. A year later, I would lose her. She committed suicide. Who even knew all the pain she bottled up!

I want you to go back to your own childhood and think of a pivotal memory!

Writing that poem began a lifestyle of journaling, and it saved my life.

Most of my childhood, I felt alone, and writing was my friend. After my mom's death, I had many questions. I didn't think I had anyone to talk to. I didn't think anyone cared. Those questions remained hidden until I had my own children.

At times, I felt like a bird molting its feathers. I was losing the old to grow new. I knew God was allowing me the time to get rid of old mindsets. My old thought patterns, my old ways of believing, my old stinking thinking. He wanted to renew my mind. I know He wants to do the same for you! The Lord was parenting me.

"I've always longed to live in a place like this, always dreamed of a room in your house, where I could sing for joy to God-alive!" (Psalms 84:2, MSG).

Writing and sitting in those quiet places, I felt a deeper stirring. God was calling me to write from head space to my heart. I felt like I was being stirred to share from the deep recesses of my heart. The Lord was calling me to new places. He wanted to take me places I had never been. I had to be willing to do things I had never done in order to have things I had never

had. I hear those same words over you. For me, it looks like one published book under my belt.

God will not push His agenda on you. He isn't all up in your face pointing His finger, screaming, "I told you so!" Your own voice might sound condemning at times. You might even hear questions like, "How did that work for you? How far did you get? Are you ready for help now, stubborn one?" No, the Lord has a loving attitude towards us.

His voice is more like, "Daughter, you got this! I know you have never done this, but I will teach you if you allow Me. I am right here with you. You are never alone! I didn't leave you then, and I am not leaving you now! I am even with you writing your book. I will use you and your story for My glory."

We also have to start somewhere. Some might call it a rough draft. If I knew how to write the book, then what fun would that be! Where would the struggle be? Who would have a great

appreciation for the small beginnings? I tend to forget about what the first time feels like. It

isn't always fun. It is rather frustrating because I am not super confident in what I am doing. I

have watched my daughter give up before wanting to try. She felt defeated before she even got

started. She was learning something new and expected to know how to do the new things.

How do you know if you have never done it before? She was learning something new, just like the times you are learning something new. As her mom, I found myself able to talk her through those times, but I wasn't always able to do the same for myself. I struggled with having confidence.

The confidence to know what I needed in the moments and the confidence to know when to ask for help. God is your parent who wants to help you! I am not always able to help myself. I am sure you feel the same. We all need a little help from time to time, even if we don't admit it. That is one of the million reasons why we need Jesus!

STORIES MATTER

To all of you authors, I am taking my hat off to you. To all of you who are writing your book, you are in good company. If I can do it, so can you! If God can walk me through the writing process,

I know He can do the same in your life. I know that most people grow weary in the process, which means they don't finish! There are so many steps to take in moving forward with any process. I could write a book on what not to do. How to not take the steps that prolong the process.

I know that my story matters. I know that your story matters! I can't wait for the connection to take place as you find your stories within my stories. I know that you are my sister from another mister. You are my brother from another mother. I want to apologize now to all you men. When I slip up and address the females, just know it isn't on purpose.

My heart cry is for women to get it! To get how much God loves them. My passion is to empower women to be all they were created to be. So, I see you, men, too! I just feel the pull towards women. I am called to empower the Beautiful Warriors.

The message of joy, wild joy, is for everyone.

Have you ever experienced someone speaking a prophetic word over you? I do hope you

say yes. If not, you are still in the right place. I want to share a cool experience. I was near the end of writing these pages and juggling many plates. My baby girl was turning the big sixteen.

For all of you, May birthdays. Mother's Day is so close to my birthday, so I decided years ago to celebrate big! I also decided I was not going to dwell on losing my mom but put my focus on being a mom. I declared the whole month to be mine. I couldn't wait for a month full of parties, dinners, special lunches, and gifts.

I might have taught my daughter that she could celebrate her whole birthday month too. Her birthday is in October, so I am tired by the time November rolls around. You know what, I don't have time to rest in November. That is a big month too! It is my anniversary month, my husband's birthday month, my sister's birthday, and it is Thanksgiving!

Back to the prophetic word. I showed up at this church service on a Thursday with much

sorrow in my heart. I might have cried on the hour car drive. I knew that I was going to a place

where I would meet Jesus. I had no desire to wipe my tears and suck it up, buttercup. I also cried almost the whole church service.

In the end, time is allotted for prophetic words. I knew I was at the right place at the right time. My heart was feeling sad, and I was in the house of the Lord. I was ready to receive! A man whom I had not met came up front, grabbed the mike, and said, "Joannie. I came here today for you. I was driving in my truck, and the Lord said, don't go home." He went on to share that he saw a vision of me being like Lucy, a sweet child in the C. S. Lewis books. He said that Lucy never wavered in her faith. She brought life wherever she went. She carried a flask of water with her. She had an enduring/special relationship with Aslan. Anytime he was around, Lucy knew it. He said, I was like Lucy, and that is how he saw my relationship with God.

He suggested I start reading *The Chronicles of Narnia.*

Wow! But, God... I needed those words more than he knew.

You better believe I went right home to look for these books. To my delight, I found six of the eight books. Who even knew? They might have been a bit worn-out paper book copies.

I remember watching *The Lion, the Witch, and the Wardrobe* with my children years

ago. I was a bit familiar with the main character Lucy because of the movie.

I want to share a few words from *The Magician's Nephew.* This was my fourth book.

Silly ole me found out this was the first one that starts the journey to Narnia. Of course, I

would be the one to read it backward. I was going off the front covers. It was very exciting to read about joy in the books. My vision for this book was right before my eyes as I turned page after page. The joy message was being confirmed!

This is what would have happened, child, with a stolen apple. It is not what will happen now. What I give you now will bring joy. It will not, in your world, give endless life, but it will heal. Go. Pluck her an apple from the tree.

C. S. Lewis, *The Magician's Nephew*

Can you believe this particular book was written in 1955? As I was reading, I thought about one of the first stories of the Bible. Adam and Eve were in a battle. They were forbidden by God not to eat from the tree of good and evil. Adam was deceived into believing he could be like God if he ate from the forbidden tree. They both ate the apple.

MANY VOICES

Do you battle with the voices in your head? Who has time to listen day after day to those annoying voices! If the voices are bringing condemnation and shame, then they are not from God! Maybe your life is full of pain because you lost sight of who the voices belong to. Is it God, is it you, or is the enemy trying to trick you? Are you going to be like Adam and disobey the voice of God? Are you going to listen to the trickery of the enemy and eat the forbidden fruit?

All the voices can cause pain and shame. If you are going to get to the other side, it is important to know. It is important to be able to identify the voice of God. The voices can cause much suffering. In our suffering, our hearts become heavy. Look around; you see heavy hearts everywhere. The world is hurting. The hearts of people everywhere are in some type of pain.

There is so much love in this world. The media wants to paint a picture that creates so much fear in the hearts of the world. I want to remind you what God wants for the world. He wants to fill your heart with love, joy, and peace!

He wants to fill your days with freedom, mercy, and grace.

Oh! May the God of green hope fill you up with joy, fill you up with peace, so that your

believing lives, filled with the life-giving energy of the Holy Spirit, will brim over with hope.

Romans 15:13 (MSG)

I pray as you read this. You are wanting change. You are seeking growth. You are

searching for more in life. Growth is part of what keeps us moving forward. When you stop

growing, you stop living. When you stop living, your choices are not about life. Your choices can quickly turn to death.

You might find yourself slipping into bad habits. As I finished up these final pages and edited my little heart out, I knew I couldn't let myself slip back into old habits. I was thinking of ways every day I could grow. What could I do differently? What areas do I need to work on? What could use some good ole growth in my life? How could I stretch myself?

You might be in that same space, asking yourself where do you need to grow. That might be why you picked up this book. Or a friend might have given you the book and is secretly thinking, you could use some growth! Ha, I am totally joking, but don't you think everyone needs to grow in areas. If that friend focuses on you, then they don't have to focus on themselves. Let that one sink in for a minute; your friend cares about you!

Pat yourself on the back; you are working on yourself. You are the only thing you can change anyway, so good job! Oh, unless you're changing diapers or a tire. LOL. I hope you will find yourself in the stories I share. I also hope you spend these next few days, weeks, or months, depending on fast you read, discovering parts of yourself. I pray you discover God. I pray you keep your focus on yourself! It is not selfish to focus on yourself.

We find days being full of dread and regret. Have you wondered why you feel sad, lonely, and depressed? It might be because you have stopped growing. It might be because your choices aren't about life, really living. They are more about not living, which can only mean a slow death. I don't think we intentionally do things to cause death. I think life can become so trying and full of loss that it becomes harder and harder to do the right thing. The right thing isn't always the easiest thing.

You might find your days to be dark and dreary. You don't even have the energy or want to have it to get out of bed. You might have even given up on yourself. I don't know where life finds you. I know where life found me, and I never want to be there again.

I pray you find your way. I don't even know your name, but I can see your sweet face.

I feel like my heart is connected to your heart even though we have never met. I pray you feel supported and celebrated. I hope you feel less alone. I want you to feel connected to a community of joy seekers. If we could all sit in a circle, I know our stories would be similar. They would all be different and unique, just like the way God made us, but we would find a thread of hope and similarities woven in them.

It is okay if you have felt like you didn't even want to wake up and face the next day. I have been there. Your fellow joy seekers have been there. At times, we wander in the wilderness. We aren't sure how long or for what reason. We need one another to find our way out. When we find our way out, we need someone who can help us not to lose our way again. Not losing my way is why Jesus has become a close companion in my adult years.

In the wild, we not only find what we are made of but who made us! We find a strength we forgot we had. We find our voice again! We find joy, that crazy wild joy that can only be discovered in the wild. I pray you will take the journey with me, that you will get your backpack ready for the adventure of your life.

I see you, I hear you. If I were with you, I would be sharing your tears. I don't know your fears, but I know mine. My heart cry is for you to discover Jesus. In doing this, you will find out

who you are. And when you know who you are, then you will know what God created you to do. Your questions about your identity will be revealed. You will tap into those weird places.

WEIRD SPACES

You don't have to be afraid. I pray once you are there, you embrace it. That you would recognize your times of struggling against God. Who is God to you? What blessings has God done for you lately? I pray you will slow down and stop struggling, stop fighting the loving arms of Jesus. He is for you, not against you.

I want you to let the thoughts of what others think to move away from you. I wasted too

many years, more than I am proud of, worrying about what others thought of me. I once heard, if they ain't gonna cry at your funeral, then what do they matter? I am just kidding when I say, "What do they matter?" But what does their opinion about your life matter?

I have learned how to be most concerned about what God thinks about my life. Even the thought, what does God think about me? How am I doing, God, with my life? Am I pleasing God with my life choices or others? Did I even do what God asked me to do? If I lived out my purpose in full capacity. Some have wondered how I do all I do. I have wondered how others do all of what they don't do. How they let the days pass them by and don't want to reach out or seek the "more." How they are able to sit comfortably in their homes and not get their hands dirty. How they have tuned out the voice of God.

In my own wild joy journey, I found out "weird" isn't the cuss word everyone thinks it is. Weird is supernatural and something that isn't normal. Why are we wasting our time trying to be so darn normal? Why try to fit in when we were made to stand out? Who wants to look the same as everyone else? Not I. At least, not anymore. What the heck does normal even mean or look like? Word! I like to think of it as a setting on a dryer. I even have a t-shirt with the print "Normal is overrated;" I believe that wholeheartedly. To be normal or not to be normal, I will take the later part.

I love this Dr. Seuss quote; I posted it on Facebook with a pic of my husband and me. I had no idea how many people would comment and resonate with it. "We're all a little weird, and life's a little weird. And when we find someone, whose weirdness is compatible with ours, we join up with them and fall in mutual weirdness and call it love."

What I do know about weird people is they are hard to forget. Don't we want to be people who are remembered? And not re-membered by what we did but what God did through us, like me writing this book?

Come on, if I can do it, then sweet sister or cool brother, so can you! So, what are you waiting for? The impossible can only be accomplished with Christ. We have to partner with God to get our life work done. It might look wild. It might look wonderful, or it might be weird. We will all have different techniques and approaches to how we live.

The way you choose to do your life work will look different than mine, and that is part of being okay with the way God made you. He made us all wild, weird, and wonderful, in my opinion. The sooner you embrace it, the quicker God can accomplish the work He is patiently waiting to do in your life. With a mindset like that, nothing or no one can stop you when you partner with the one who created you! Let's pull up our sleeves and grab that God-fidence God has packed up for you.

CHAPTER 3:
Yes, Jesus, Yes

Whatever God has promised gets stamped with the Yes of Jesus.

2 Corinthians 1:20 (MSG)

Do I have any "Yes, Jesus, yes" people holding this book? The ones who know that they know Jesus has stamped His "yes" on their lives! The ones who are willing to wander in the wilderness. Now let me preface this by saying the wilderness isn't always a bad thing. I can tell you. I think I spent half of my life in the wilderness. Did I have moments where I questioned God? Absolutely! Did I want to throw my hands up in the air and camp out until...

Until I was picked up and thrown out.

Until I was plucked up and thrown out.

The wilderness is where the wild ones find joy. The wild ones are the ones who don't want to miss a thing! The ones who are wild in their yes!

The crazy ones who don't always weigh the cost and say, "Yes!" A yes before you have time to think about what is being asked of you. A yes that only came because of your no. No matters as much as your yes! As my teenage daughter would say, "That would be a hard no, Mom!" Did you know that no is a complete sentence?

I read years ago, if you hesitate in your answer, then listen to your body. Your body is telling you, think really hard about saying yes. I have learned through the years that when I am constantly saying yes to others, I leave little space to tell myself yes. Anyone else struggled with telling yourself no? Ya gotta create that space to say yes, to you.

Shall we dive into the times God is asking a question? What is your first response? You can be honest, is it a no because you are so busy or a bit afraid?

What is God asking you to do? Are you waiting for some pie in the sky to come down and confirm it? He might have given you signs or symbols, but you missed them because they didn't look like what you thought they would.

I have a sweet friend like a sister who would always end her conversations with, "If it's the Lord's will, I will see you later or talk to you soon." I never understood what she meant by saying that, "If the Lord's will." I was so wrapped in trying to live in my own will. I didn't grow up in church. God's will, what does that even mean?

I figured out; God had a will for my life. God has a will for your life too! Let me say this before you get all squirming like I was when my friend said, "If the Lord is willing." God will not force His will on His children. He takes many opportunities to present His will to you. I missed many opportunities; I didn't trust God or His will.

When is the last time you slowed down? Maybe you did an inventory of your life; where are you? Is this where you want to be? How many opportunities have you missed because you picked your will over God's will? I need to ask again, do you even know what that means, God's will. God has a will for you!

Let's get real; fear can stop you from living in God's will. How many times did you say no because of fear? I can answer that for you, too many!

I also am grateful for the "yes, Jesus" moments. I have accomplished some scary stuff you could say was God's will because I know Jesus had my back. I am grateful that I didn't let being afraid keep me from life-changing experiences.

Let's share and tell time. Remember the good ole school days where we had show and tell? This is a bit different scenario, you are at your home, and I am at my home, so we will share separately but together. The sharing will involve memories, not things.

We will share times you didn't feel equipped like you were the right person. The times you didn't know how it was all going to work out. If God is in your life, then you might not know how but you knew who! You know who is sharing a new thing for you to do? God is the who, and He is sharing plus telling you. He is telling you what will bring your heart joy and fulfillment. In your relationship with God, show and tell can look like God giving you a vision for something He is asking you to do.

I will start with sharing. The Lord told my husband and me to do a youth camp in our backyard. Not only have we never done that before, but we haven't even heard of it being done. When I was talking to God about it, He was reminding me that it was okay; I didn't know what to do. If I let Him, He would show me and teach me.

All I know is my teens have some awesome friends, and I wanted to be a part of their lives. The doors to attend camp were closing, and I was praying for an open door of opportunity. I knew that if I didn't find an open door, then I would create my own way. I know that sounds scary, and it was! As I am writing this, camp is only eleven days away! I woke up early to hear from the Lord. He had provision and fresh manna for me. How many times are we okay with the manna from yesterday? We aren't always willing to sacrifice a bit of our time for God.

I knew, in this situation, I had to hear from God.

SEEKING BREAKTHROUGH

I was fasting and asking for a breakthrough. I woke up that Monday morning with conflicting thoughts. I am not an anxious person, but this day, I was. I was questioning myself and my yes.

I heard myself saying, "Like you know what you are doing, Joannie! As if you needed one more thing to add to your life. Why would you even consider trying to put together a youth camp?" Yes, those accusing voices were tormenting me. I knew this wasn't God, and it wasn't me. I am a fun-loving lady most of the time! I look for challenges and exciting opportunities.

What voices are you listening to? In this season of your life, what voice is louder? Who are you listening to? The loving voice of Jesus cheering you on or a voice like fingernails on the chalkboard condemning you. Are you feeling positive about what you are doing or down and out? I can identify better now what voice I am listening to. It is only because I have been in a relationship with Jesus for many, many years. Jesus revealed himself to me as a friend. He is calling you friend too!

James was a man that God called friend, and he was called God's friend. What does this mean to you? Is this a breakthrough you have been waiting for? Have you been praying for a friend, a real friend? A friend draws close to you; a friend wants you close to them.

"Come near to God and he will come near to you" (James 4:8, NIV).

In the spring of 2019, I attended an Elvis impersonating event with a young lady who was like my older daughter. Her mom was also a huge Elvis lover. It meant a lot to share the event with her! This was a big deal because I have been a fan of Elvis since I was in the womb. I remember my mom playing "Hound Dog," "Blue Suede Shoes," "Jailhouse Rock" all the time. She loved Elvis! Her love for Elvis was a gift she passed down to me.

The short years I had with my mom, I grew to love Elvis. If I am honest, I remember dance parties in our small trailer. Music soothes our soul, and it brings happiness. Sometimes, you have so much hurt in your heart that the space is too cluttered to remember the good. I know there had to be lots of good memories with my mom. Her death, the loss of my mother left me wanting to block it all out.

I don't think I wanted to remember anything. How do you process? Your mom left you? She checked out. She didn't want to live anymore. I mean, as a little girl, I didn't! I only thought, if I don't think about her, then maybe my heart won't hurt so bad. Maybe not remembering will mean the memories will go away. Those thoughts kept me forgetting until my adult years. As an adult, I started unlocking memories of my mom. Memories that we locked up for decades!

I want to reassure you that the good memories are worth remembering. We are all on our own journey; you take your time. God is waiting for you to ask Him to help you remember.

To feel, to live, to remember.

It took a lot for me to even share with you the connection between Elvis and my mom. I am so grateful for my sweet friend, who read my manual and gave me honest feedback. She could sense I was holding back and sensed I still had issues in my heart. I told her she was right! I was a bit mad at my mom, and maybe I would share more in another book. At that time, I didn't have much to share about my mom.

I get it! I have done the same thing with losing loved ones. I learned. Over time, in the healing, you will start to remember. Be kind to yourself, ask this of yourself, do you want to remember? I don't want to forget who my loved ones once were. I can honestly say that at this season in my life. I don't want to forget my mom, who I knew her to be, who God made her, to fade away. We are talking 1986 is how long it has been since my mom took her life.

I didn't see myself smiling like a happy little girl during those dance parties. I also don't see myself sad. I saw a little girl who was enjoying her mom. I am sure I was hoping those times wouldn't end. As you know, good times do eventually end. You wouldn't be able to experience new memories if they didn't. I had no clue those memories would only last twelve years. The memories of my mom didn't last long. I am so grateful my mom passed down her love for all music, especially Elvis! Her other favorite music was country! My daughter loves to jam out to country songs too. She sure didn't learn it from me!

I am glad, as an adult, I have these sweet memories to reflect on and share with my children. I actually think my son looks like Elvis. Did you know his birthday was on January 8, and he had a twin brother, Jesse, who was born first but died at birth? His mom said it was tragic to lose one son but glorious because the other one lived and was bound for greatness. She later told Elvis, "The one who lives gets the strength of both." And when he first started singing, people described him as a "howling hillbilly." I have never heard that term until I was doing research for this book. My sister-in-law bought me a book, *Remembering Elvis: 30 Years Later*, published by Life.

Can you believe Elvis received his first guitar at eleven years old? He took it to school with him. He was always playing the guitar. Can you imagine rock and roll today if it wasn't for Elvis stepping into his greatness? What if he wouldn't have gotten the guitar as a gift? What if he didn't start playing it? A great thing to remember, his roots in music was gospel music.

No matter what you believe about him, I am a fan! It is hard to admit, but my (second) daughter, who was at the event with me, is a bigger Elvis fan than I am! Her mom bought her ticket as a Christmas gift. The event was at a local theatre. It was a small theatre but had the capacity to hold hundreds of people.

In between all the Elvis songs, I saw myself on the stage speaking where the Elvis impersonator was singing. I know it sounds a bit wild and crazy, but it is a true story. I asked God several times if He was sure about this location. What was I going to be speaking about? I surely wasn't going to be doing plays. I wrote the vision down in my journal.

It took me a few weeks before I started pursuing this vision which would turn into a God dream. You can't call it anything but a dream with God in the middle of it. I knew I was not going to pull this one off without Him. I needed next steps of what to do. First of all, who did I talk to?

God made this dream a reality. In May 2019, I hosted my first women's event, Ignite. It happened! I did not pull it off alone. It took a team to believe in my vision. I had to ask for help. Thankfully I had some amazing women in my life who said yes to my crazy vision.

Y'all need to get you some of those kinds of people, the ones who have your back! I will never forget all the hard work put into making that event happen—lots of lessons learned. If I would have second-guessed everything, then the event wouldn't have happened! I did not know what I was doing. Sometimes the hardest part is starting. I just did what I felt God was asking me to do. He had a message for me to share about "identity."

FOLLOW YOUR DREAMS

I was exhausted and could barely keep my eyes open. My husband suggested we put one of those romance movies. I knew his plan, to go to sleep. I figured I would be asleep before him. Not so fast. I am a sucker for romance movies with a twist, especially if I can trust the channel; it was on UPtv from 2016. If I start a movie, then I have to see how it ends.

Just in case I went to sleep, my eye mask was ready to don. I dozed a few times but was awakened by the characters and curious about the dad in the movie.

I know God wanted to meet with me in the quiet of the night. The only sound I heard was the ceiling fan squeaking. I was not expecting to be caught up with emotions, but I was. A few times, I couldn't stop the tears from flowing. Part of the story had to do with relationships between a child and father.

I was missing my own dad. He was gone a day and eleven months. Some days it felt longer, and other days, my heart was only tracing a few days or weeks. I couldn't even believe I was coming up on the year mark.

It is hard for a heart to feel the grief. My life was full of loss and pain. I thought this movie would bring me cheer, not tears. I am not going to tell you all the juicy details, but I do want to share a few lines from the movie.

"Follow your dreams. Give it your best shot. You never have to live with any regrets.

I am proud of you" (*Love Throws a Curve*).

This was between a father and son. I want all of you to picture your heavenly Father saying this to you.

What are you waiting to do but scared to death? Death like you are frozen in fear. Has fear caused you to stop trying? Are you rehearsing lies that might sound something like this, "What is the point anyways? Why even try because I am going to fail."

I got so stirred up watching this movie, *Love Throws a Curve*. I had to find my computer and capture these thoughts for you.

Do you know what I believe the most important four words are?

I believe in you!

After losing my mom at such a young age, I decided I was going to dedicate the rest of my life to believe in others. And I mean "fiercely" believing, especially in women. I would keep believing until I started seeing signs that they were believing in themselves. I think this passion came from growing up without a parent to believe in me. I graduated high school by the grace of God. I wanted it; I wanted to be different. Another one of those "but God" moments!

I wasn't the girl who set goals. I didn't know much about goals. All I knew was my parents were high school dropouts, and I wasn't going to be anything like them!

I wanted my story to be about a girl who pushed through all the obstacles and graduated. I wanted a high school graduation party. I wanted the joy of walking to get my diploma. I thought the white robes were cool. I graduated with over 400 people; it was a big event. I had to

believe in myself to get to that graduation.

Who attends ten different schools, not being a military family? I know some of you can add a few more schools to the list. My children only went to one public school and a few private schools. Josie was in my belly, and Seth was a year old when we moved to our Montgomery home. I only heard stories about living in the same place for more than five years.

The one thing I lacked was security growing up, and I wanted to give my children a sense of security. It is so important to feel secure. On my arm and ankle, you would find an anchor tattoo. Anchors have always represented security and a foundation of faith to me.

I was sad to see my siblings not finish school. I wondered many times how different their lives could have been. If only they had parents to raise them and push them to graduate. I didn't have it, but I had God. I don't know all the details, and I am not trying to say they didn't have anyone to believe in them. I know my dad did the best he could with his own childhood pain.

GOT BELIEF

I wanted to dig a bit differently into what exactly belief means. Believe comes from the old German words, meaning to trust. Belief doesn't require proof, just acceptance.

You have to believe in yourself before you can believe in others. Or is it? Do you believe that to be true? Or would you say it is much easier to believe in others before your own self? Do you think it takes someone else to believe in you before you can start to believe in yourself? This feels like a riddle, and I feel it will be a lifetime for us to explore.

To believe or not to believe. What are your beliefs, and why do you believe what you do? Have you ever had the courage to question your beliefs? I think this is what happened to my friend, the one I said no longer believed in Jesus. She dissected her beliefs and didn't know how

to put them back together again. There was a big hole when it came to the faith department. She

didn't believe what she once believed, and she was left with not knowing how she believed about God.

It makes me sad to think God is the one who always gets picked on. Now, it is up to

her to seek the pieces that are missing to put her faith back together again. I also believe God doesn't leave us in those times of brokeness. Reminding me of the nursery rhyme, Humpty Dumpty. "Humpty Dumpty sat on a wall, Humpty Dumpty had a great fall, All the king's horses and all the king's men couldn't put Humpty together again."

It is funny how we still try to do it all on our own to include putting ourselves back together.

I don't think I ever questioned if my faith was broken. I more than likely made up for it, wondering, "Am I broken?" There were many, many years when I believed God was the only one whom I thought loved me and believed in me. The adults in my life didn't protect me and left me to figure out my pain. This made me feel broken.

I know there have been times that I have wondered why I believe what I believe. I am reassured and know that I don't have to have this larger-than-life belief. God's Word says we only need faith the size of a mustard seed. I take this truth seriously. If all I need is a mustard seed, then we are good to go!

Believing in others is one of the most amazing gifts a dad holds. So much space for support, encouragement, and love. I shared that my dad spent a lifetime overcoming his addictions. I know he loved me. I will say I questioned his love for me a lot! But the day he took his last breath, I was secure that my dad loved me!

Maybe, you didn't know your dad or have that assurance about his love. This, my sweet readers, is why I could scream off the roof tops, *your* heavenly Father is madly, deeply, and passionately in love with you! His love is so big, so wide, so deep. He can't get enough of you!

DREAM TIME

Dreams can be what we follow, and they can be what follows us. God has been speaking to me in my dreams for years. I used to be tormented by nightmares. I didn't know much about the power of Jesus; I could actually pray over myself. I know I could write a whole book on

dreaming at night with God. I do want to take the time to share one recurring dream with you.

If you are not remembering your dreams when you go to sleep, you can ask God to help you remember them. God has answered some huge questions in my dream life. The answers do not always come clearly, but they come in a way for you to seek more. God sets us up to go on a

journey of finding what symbols, signs, and people you dream about mean.

Have you ever had one of those dreams where you didn't want to wake up? I am so

serious when I tell you that I had the same dream, three different endings. Every time I went back to sleep, I was in the same dream, but the ending changed. The Lord showed me in this dream that I had the power. I knew what was coming. What if this was real life? We knew what was to come! We knew the ways of the enemy! We were more prepared for the attacks. The battles that we won caused us to be battle-ready.

"Who is this King-Glory? God, armed and battle-ready"
(Psalm 24:8, MSG).

I was a spiritual assassin in this dream. I am not even kidding when I tell you that I twisted the head off of the bad person in my dream. I am not a violent person but God… It reminded me that sometimes we forget who God made us to be. We let life knock us down. We drop without a real fight. As you might remember, in battle, back in the day, you didn't show up for a fight without your sword.

Why did you put your sword down? Have you lost your sword or let your sword collect dust? Better yet, do you even own a sword? One of my Beautiful Warrior friends bought me my first sword. It was the best gift a warrior woman could receive! I have learned the significance of the sword. It is a weapon to fight darkness and evils ways of the enemy. God's Word has become my greatest weapon.

There are three *Wonder Woman* pictures nicely hung above my sword. I was a bit scared to hang my sword up; who wants to have it accidentally fall on their head? I need the visual and daily reminder. I also need to remember what God says about me.

He calls me a warrior woman. He sees me as a wonder woman. He calls me to do extraordinary things in this world. He also calls you! How will you answer His call? Will it be a "Yes, Jesus, yes"? I am so thankful I don't have to wear a wonder woman costume or carry a sword to be fearless, and neither do you. Although, it would be kind of cool. LOL.

CHAPTER 4:
Fearless Ones

Be strong and take heart, all you who hope in the Lord.

Psalm 31:24 (NIV)

I also see you, wild ones. The ones who were told, "You won't amount to anything." The ones who the world/society might have given up on. It's okay because God has you! You aren't holding this book by chance. I don't only see you, I know you. I am one of you! I felt most of my life that I was too much. I was told that I needed to dial it down a few notches. Listening to these voices, I found that I lost parts of who I was. I tried to be what others wanted me to be. I am who I am, as you are who you are! You do not have another carbon copy. The Lord's freedom sets you on a path to fully embrace all parts of yourself.

My past is not spotless. I didn't grow up believing in Jesus. I grew up with a spirit of fear that haunted me in my waking and my sleeping hours. I feel like my mind was constantly wondering if the adults in my life were going to leave me. I didn't know who was going to be home when I got off the school bus. I barely remember any hot meals shared around the table. I don't know if my mom even had a kitchen table.

She did the best she could. I never had to worry about food. I have memories of taking food stamps into the grocery store. It seemed like a fun thing then; to buy what I wanted. I knew my family didn't have much, but when my Mom was alive, I knew she loved me. She cared for my siblings and me the best way she knew how. She was raised by an alcoholic father who was abusive. Why would I be surprised that she dated men who thought it was okay to hit her and call her degrading names.

I wish I could tell that beautiful lady, "Momma, you are doing a great job raising those four babies all by yourself." I wish I could tell my mom, "You are an awesome woman, and God has big plans for you. Don't ever stop believing in yourself. I know it is hard now, but it won't be forever."

I wish I would have been older so I could have had a heart-to-heart with my mom. I know at twelve, I didn't have any answers. I did accept Jesus at eleven years old. He made me fearless even in my fear. When I said "I do" to Jesus, everything changed on the inside. Can I tell you that everything changed? No way! I mean, not even a year later is when my mom died. What is a young girl to think about God? The woman who brought me into this world is gone. How can God love me? It wouldn't be until many years later that I would fully receive His unconditional love.

WILD MEMORIES

There are memories that still haunt me. I know people have hurt you and let you down. Believe me when I tell you I feel your pain. I do have some good news for you! This is what

God says about being wild. God loves His wild women! God loves you! God loves me, and God loved my mom. He also loves you, wild men.

"Be here—the king is wild for you. Since he's your lord, adore him" (Psalm 45:11, (MSG).

The day finally came when my daughter was asked to be a girlie friend!

A what?

A girlfriend? My fifteen-year-old daughter, a what did you

say? Yes, this was all happening to remind me to let her go and allow her to spread those wings she was growing.

We were not even comfortable with the boy crushes. I knew we were going to need a lot of Jesus to embrace a boyfriend. This young man in Josie's life started out as a huge blessing, and then not! As the months went on, she thought she was so in love and talked about marriage. My family grew to love him too. We tried to give them opportunities to get to know each other. It was not easy, but I trusted God. What I couldn't see ahead of us was the trials and hurt to come.

I wished, as her mom, that I would have trusted my gut more. I sure did a lot of praying! I was surprised by the triggers that kept coming up! The triggers were things God wanted me to deal with because when God reveals it, He wants to heal it. I had to focus on all the healing I received, and this was Josie's relationship, not mine! It was a daily struggle to trust this young man with my daughter. She was navigating through new waters. My whole family was chartering those new waters too. It was fresh, new territory for my family. I was leaning into God and trying not to let my past hurts infiltrate into her dating life.

I honestly was not ready for her to date, but she was almost sixteen, and she thought she was ready. I knew I needed to let her date while she was still living at home. I didn't want her to date until she was thirty. That seemed like a great number to pick. LOL. Ultimately, Josie had to make her own mistakes as she tried on this whole girlfriend role. Funny looking back, parents make a lot of mistakes too, wearing the "my daughter is dating" role.

We finally said yes, and I share more about why we said yes. One memorable good time was when her new boyfriend brought Josie a dozen red roses. This was the day he asked her to homecoming. Unfortunately, the event didn't happen because of the annoying COVID.

A bit of a warning, parents, when something seems a bit too good to be true, it more than likely is. Watch for the signs even when you think everything seems good.

This book was written in 2020 and finished in the late spring of 2021. What else was there to do in that long year of COVID! Ha, I spent my time writing, writing, and more writing. It is a time in history no one will ever forget. I hope that you made good memories as well as the unexpected and not-so-good ones that we all tried to deal with. I can say Josie dating that year came with its own set of complications.

We still made incredible memories as a family, even in the midst of those complications. I want to honor my daughter and not share too much about her personal life. My family would find ourselves in unchartered territory as Josie dated. We struggled with the breaking up part the most. No one saw it coming; I am sure Josie did near the end. I cried out to God many times. Lord, we didn't know how to do this dating thing, and we sure don't know how to do this breaking up thing.

There were so many lessons for my family to learn during that time. I am only going to share a few of them. I was blessed to witness how my husband handled his baby girl dating. He took charge! I was impressed and honored to be his wife. There were three questions that stood out to me the most.

First of all, Tim asked him what it meant to have a girlfriend. I will say that he stumbled over his words a bit. He said, "I don't really know how to say it." Tim said, "I am not looking for a Webster dictionary definition." He said, "What does it mean to you?" He said, "Well, you know she is the only one I like. You know I like, like her." Tim said, "I know what you mean. You like, like her." It was the cutest and felt like after hearing the conversation, we could trust this young boy.

Looking back, I can see where we might have trusted a little too much. I don't think either one of them, the boy or Josie, were ready for a serious relationship. My heart was joyful getting to witness how my husband handled himself as Josie's dad.

Tim also brought up these three areas that many of you might recognize if you know anything about the military. I know you are wondering what was discussed, but as I mentioned before, I want to honor my daughter. You might read more about it in my next book. Wink wink.

1. Honor.

2. Respect.

3. Protect.

What do these words mean to you? Honor, what comes to mind when you say it out loud? Respect, is that something you do for others or for yourself? Protect, what does that mean to you? Josie's dating turned out to be one of the greatest parenting lessons.

If I could go back, I would have said no and dealt with the teenage attitude. I guess one of the ways you learn is to make a bunch of mistakes. Life is one big lesson at a time. The lesson is to not do life without God. We thought we heard from God.

I feel some things in life are personal and sacred. They are to be experienced and not always shared with others, but I share some details to help others along the way.

What kind of stories do you have? What details do you wish you would have known about dating or relationships in general? "Honor, respect, and protect" apply to all your relationships. I want to remind you of the one who will always exemplify this to you! His name is Jesus. He will never let you down. Jesus will always honor, respect, and protect you. Did you know God is concerned mostly with your heart?

HEART ISSUES

"So above all, guard the affections of your heart, for they affect all that you are. Pay attention to the welfare of your innermost being, for from there flows the wellspring of life" (Proverbs 4:23, TPT).

There are days, you ask, do I trust my heart? Will my heart

lead me astray, or is my heart the one thing I can count on, or will I betray me? The whole dating season left my heart broken; it felt like into many pieces. I was reminded, time and time again, how I felt as a young girl. Thankfully, in those young years, I created the lifestyle of journaling. You better believe I used up my journal in a month. In all that journaling, I somehow found the words to describe what my heart was feeling. I will try my best to share them with you.

I felt like my heart was being ripped apart. I was felt like my heart was crying. I felt like tears were pouring out of my heart, and I didn't know how to stop them! I knew I was feeling that way because someone I loved very much was hurting. I knew I couldn't change the situation, but I still didn't have to like it. It had a lot to do with my daughter's breakup and all the first experiences of her life.

I didn't know how to let go and let God be God. He is the healer of all hearts! I was in desperate need of my heart being healed. The whole dating thing for my daughter was new and her heart being broken was new for our family. The healing needed wasn't just for me but also for her. I was having a hard time carrying my burdens, and it was weighing me down as I tried to carry hers too.

I wasn't even asking God to take it away. I was doing a little bit of wallowing in it. I will admit; eventually, I did ask God for help because my shoulders were feeling super heavy. I no longer wanted to carry it and wanted to lay it all down, all the hurt, all the pain, all the heartbreak I was experiencing.

What a wonderful time to be going to counseling. I needed someone with professional experience to talk to. My therapist was like a friend at this time. We had over two long hard years together. I love how no matter what I was going through, she would tell me I was doing a good job because I was putting in the work.

Sometimes we want things to change, including ourselves but don't want to do the necessary work. The work is where we find transformation. And the work isn't as grueling when we partner with God. He's the one who will carry the majority of it all.

Have you ever had those situations; you couldn't get them out of your head; the details. I'm telling you, this dating season tried to take me out! I am not even being dramatic. There was a bunch of trusting I had to do. I had to trust God, I had to trust Josie, I had to trust the boy, I had to trust my husband, and then I had to trust myself. Oh my.... trust was already an area I needed work in.

It was so hard to let Josie out of my sight. I wanted to lock her in her bedroom and say, I changed my mind. "Nope, we aren't going to let you date." I don't think that would have gone well. Josie was still living at home, and it seemed like a good time to let her try on the dating thing. I had to remember; God loves her way more than I ever could. That is a hard pill to swallow. I had to trust that God was on the scene! A saying I would find myself quoting over and over. God is on the scene! I felt a huge battle brewing. I knew it was a battle I was not going to fight alone. I needed God, and I needed others.

I needed my battle buddy warriors to carry me through it. I needed renewed hope that things would change, that the heart-break would end! I needed to hear this was not the end of the story!

I just happen to be scrolling through channels on TV, searching high and low for something decent to watch! I caught a glimpse of a movie I love and could quote parts of it. The timing was right on because this was a week before the bad news I received. Can I just tell you it was one of my favorites? Any of you heard of this 1998 flick? I will share a few quotes from the movie first and see if you know. Don't look ahead until you make at least one guess (please).

> Childhood is what you spend the rest of your life trying to overcome. That's what Momma always says. She says that beginnings are scary, endings are usually sad, but it's the middle that counts the most. Try to remember that when you find yourself at a new beginning. Just give hope a chance to float up. And it will,

too.

Okay, if that didn't jog your memory, then what about this? "Dancing is just a conversation between two people. Talk to me."

I DARE YOU TO BE FEARLESSLY YOU!

This word, fearless, was one of the last tattoos I got. One might look at me and think, *Why does this sweet lady have ink marked upon her body*. I have ink because I am an artist at heart. I believe our bodies are temples that will one day perish. The only thing we will have left is our spirit, and it will be enjoying a new heaven and a new earth. The ink on our bodies will be gone, just like everything else.

A year and a few months after my dad's death, I got a new tattoo, "pearl"! The COVID epidemic delayed this tattoo. I wanted to honor my dad with the word "pearl" in his handwriting. I also found a feather in watercolors. My dad was one of the only people who called me by my middle name. Okay, now you know my middle name. I used to think I would pass it down to my daughter but decided on Hope, and that fits her. Pearl is my grandmother's middle name. I am grateful to carry it on. You would think I was born in the south, but nope, I guess God knew I was destined to live in the south and raise my babies in Alabama. It still blows my mind to think I have southern children with my southern man!

The sweetest story to share with you about my "pearl" tattoo. I was ecstatic the day I showed it to my grandmother. My grandmother Benton was battling her own health issues. Any day I got a chance to visit her was a darn good day! Y'all, I can't even make this up when I tell you she was glowing. Her face lit up when I got close to show "pearl" to her. I was watching her, her mind coming and going; some call it Alzheimer's. I call it a nasty joke played! On the visit, sweet grandmother didn't know who I was. She just looked at me. She said, "Well, you are pretty." I said, "Thank you, Grandma." I was praying about if I would bring up my dad.

I knew she missed her son so much! I felt the leading of

the Holy Spirit to say, "Grandma, I am Joannie, Chuck's oldest daughter." When I said that to her, she started crying. I saw tears in her eyes, and all I knew to do was hug her so tight! We embraced for what felt like ten minutes, but I knew only a few. It was the sweetest hug. I showed her my tattoo, and I said, "Grandma, look, I have your name on my arm. That is my name too. I am the oldest, and your son named me after you. She got the biggest grin on her face, and I had my grandma back. She then showed me one she had. I have seen it many times. I said, "I know, Grandma." She said, "Who's name is that?" I said, "That was your old boyfriend." LOL.

I will treasure that visit in my heart as a joyous adventure. I sat as close to her as I could. I let her talk all she wanted about my dad, her Chuck. I kept thinking, *Is this going to be the last time I get to see her alive? Lord, let me not miss a thing!*

Back to my fearless tattoo. In one of my encounters at church, a man commented on my tattoo as I walked up front for prayer. I thought, *I know, he is going to be judgy pants and tell me how wrong I am for getting it,* nope! I was wrong. He asked me if God was involved. I said, "Yes, of course. I got this one in Texas. Two other friends and I got them the same night. We wanted to get matching tattoos. The word fearless with an arrow." He said, "Well, the Lord was involved, and this is how He sees you. He sees you fearless."

I want to remind you too.

He sees you fearless!

Do you believe that? I get tripped up sometimes and don't believe it, to be honest with you. There is no shame in wondering. A lesson in those times of wonder, I discovered the wonder!

Another great lesson I learned that day. Who was the judgy pants? It wasn't him; it was me for thinking he was going to judge me. God loves us, but He will use moments like that to check yourself! Yep, we all need a good check from time to time—better known as those humble pie-eating days.

Do I have any dove lovers? You know those tasty little chocolates wrapped in silver foil with encouraging messages. The night I was working on my rough draft, I needed a pick me up. My husband was out of town for work. My teenagers drove off into the wild blue yonder. Not really, but they did drive off to a football game in my truck. I was a bit more concerned about my vehicle, Black Beauty, than my long-legged teens! I am kidding. I can't imagine my life without my precious G babes. "G babes" is the name I started calling them years ago. Don't even ask; some people on Facebook get confused thinking I was talking about grandbabies. Now that is funny business. The message I got from my dove chocolate was, "Be fearlessly authentic."

Did any of you guess the movie I referenced? Okay, Okay, I will tell you the title, *Hope Floats*! Yes, starring Sandra Bullock and Harry Conick Jr. They are two of my favorites. A woman who can make a fool of herself on film, in *Miss Congeniality*. I know she got paid high dollars but still. I can relate to a woman who doesn't take herself too seriously.

Congrats to those of you who picked the movie! As I edited, I was stirred up to watch *Hope Floats* again. Who has the popcorn and water or soda for you pop drinkers? Yes, I said "pop," a bit of my Indiana roots showing. My husband likes to make fun of me and call me a darn "Yankee." At least I'm his Yankee wife. Hey, he is the one who married me!

Since this chapter was all about being fearless, if you are alive, then you need to say this out loud, "I am fearless!" I think everyone needs to take a pause, a selah moment, and just speak that over themselves.

I am fearless!

CHAPTER 5:
Freedom Riders

Christ has set us free to live a free life. So take your stand! Never again let anyone put a harness of slavery on you.

Galatians 5:1 (MSG)

No, in all these things we are more than conquerors through him who loved us.

Romans 8:37 (NIV)

One sunny winter morning, my family and I were awakened to the sound of motorcycle

engines revving. The sound was so close I knew it had to be coming from a place very, very close to us. I was going to investigate! I didn't want to seem like the super nosey neighbor, so I came up with a plan. Y'all know, you gotta act like you are doing something other than being nosey. I went to the mailbox with a card in hand.

It is always a good day to send a word of encouragement to a friend. Standing at the mailbox, I casually peeked to my right. I saw a bunch of people dressed in black and red clothing. It was a beautiful sight. My view was people and motorcycles. A lot of motorcycles, I might add. These sharp-dressed men gathered around their bikes in black suits with red shirts. The ladies had on red dresses. My first thought was, *Oh no, someone died, and this is a family gathering for a funeral.*

My teens already deemed this house a family vacation home.

We only saw vehicles in the

driveway on holidays. The only people we ever saw were teenagers. The details really don't matter, do they? Or do they matter more than we admit at times because, when we don't have the details, we tend to make up stories? We have a perception of what we see. Just a little something to think about as I finish my story.

The whole trust your gut thing was coming up. My gut told me it was a funeral gathering. This was 2020, the year COVID and face masks. Our pictures are going to be funny when we are sharing them with our grandchildren.

The sound of the bikes revving made my husband want to ride. I said, "Babe, get on your

bike and join them!" He knows I am the crazy one who would do it, but he wasn't about that. He

was happy standing in the driveway from afar. I wanted to get up in all that action and find out

what and why they were preparing for a funeral procession.

He went through a bit of a mid-life crisis and bought an Indian bike for his big fiftieth

birthday that same year. I said, "Babe, go ride and have fun." I told him I would give him a report on what happened next door. He said he was curious but wanted to ride more. I guess he wanted to feel the wind blowing his hair. That is funny because he is bald. LOL.

I tried to keep my eye on what was going on next door. An hour later, I heard more engines reviving and then a few police vehicles. I knew then my suspicions were on point. I was sadly right in thinking someone had passed away.

My husband came home just as the lineup for the funeral procession was starting. We

were honored to watch the lineup of riders while chilling on our front porch. My daughter was inside and took a short video. Most teenagers are armed and ready with a camera for opportunities like this! I am not kidding when I tell y'all my husband counted seventeen motorcycles.

I couldn't contain my emotions anymore. The tears were rolling down my face. I completely lost it when the white hearse pulled up. I dotted my tears with my hands and thought, *What is wrong with you, woman?* It was a moment I didn't want to miss. The respect, the honor, the love, and the work that was put into this funeral procession. I could feel the love from my porch. The fist bumps, handshakes, and hugs shared by grown men in black leather jackets would be forever engraved in my mind. It was a tender moment.

My heart was feeling the love and the loss. Y'all might think I am crazy, and that is okay, cause news flash, I can be a crybaby. When my family makes fun of me, I remind them I am alive! I am not numbing my pain with substance abuse. I am feeling my feelings, and my heart is open. This usually gets a holy hush out of them. That January morning was no different. A few cars followed behind the bikes, and then they were gone. It was a beautiful sight with much honor to witness especially so up close and personal.

I remembered my chapter about freedom and knew this was a story I didn't want to miss

sharing with you.

In the year 2020, an online community was very popular. It kept neighborhoods

informed and neighbors connected! Connected neighbors. The next day of this funeral, I saw a message from the owner of the home next to me stating her parents had passed away. She wanted to give a warning to her neighborhood. I find it funny. She stated a couple of motorcycles would be there. We counted seventeen, and you can only imagine that sound. It was glorious to witness. This sweet lady shared that she lost her mom to COVID at the beginning of December. Then she lost her dad a few weeks later. I was undone!

What a tragedy for the family. She stated her parents were married over fifty years! Wow, no wonder I felt such love and respect as I watched the lineup. I prayed about meeting this sweet woman and sharing with her how much the funeral procession meant to me. I was still grieving the loss of my dad. I was hoping to hear more about her relationship with her parents. I wanted to be able to tell her face to face how sorry I was for her dear loss. I wouldn't get the opportunity because a few weeks later, she was moved out and was long gone! I still can't believe she lived next door for two years, and I didn't get the chance to meet her.

How is that even possible? I had never met her. A reality check of where life was in 2020. A reminder that being closed in our homes wasn't working for the world. A reminder of how everyone was so busy and didn't take time to chat with their neighbors. I bet she

was the beautiful lady in the red dress with the hat on?

WILD AND FREE

Wild is all about being free! You were born to live in freedom! Remember the 1969 song by Steppenwolf, "Born to be Wild." I want to share a few lyrics with you.

> Get your motor runnin'
>
> Head out on the highways
>
> Lookin' for adventure
>
> And whatever comes our way
>
> Yeah Darlin' go make it happen
>
> Take the world in a love embrace
>
> …Born to be wild
>
> Born to be wild

If you go back and watch the video, grown men are riding their motorcycles down

the highway. If you continue to watch, you will see them doing tricks on their bikes. It wasn't

enough for them to just be riding; they were having fun and taking risks! What a fun, wild ride making that video.

Ladies—it is a hot sight to see your man who is aged with that salt and pepper look on a motorcycle! Well, I shall confess, my man is bald and doesn't have much hair but don't think for one minute that bald isn't beautiful because it is! I got my bald man, so y'all gonna have to find your own. Seriously, as I write this, my bald-headed bike-riding husband turned the big fifties, as I shared earlier. I will tell ya, the older he gets, the finer he becomes. Let's not be so shallow; not just about his look; it is because of his attitude, servanthood, and faith. I can see the growth and fire in his eyes for the more that Jesus died for. To all my single ladies, let thy hope be renewed in finding your wild man who loves Jesus. To all my married ladies, tell that man of yours how much you love him and how hot he is to you. You never know what you might spark.

Are you still having fun in your life? Did your wild ways make you better person or worse person? Wild doesn't have to be a bad thing. We can be wild for the things of God. When you look in the mirror, who do you see? What do you see? Do you see an expression of freedom looking back at you? Or do you see a bound-up person? Are you looking at someone who has lots of regrets and has been afraid to really live?

I used to look in the mirror and only see my mistakes mixed with shame, guilt, and

remorse. I was not always proud of the woman looking back at me. The days of being wild

without Jesus led to decisions without any boundaries. I didn't know how to respect myself.

I might have accepted Jesus in my heart at an early age, but what did that mean. I will share more about my salvation in another chapter. I can tell you, I was not living my life for Jesus, and honestly, I didn't know how. I still had a lot of mistakes to make. Wouldn't you agree, mistakes are the best teacher? I feel you get tripped up when you keep making the same mistakes. Our mistakes are to learn from and hopefully not make again. This has been part of the wild joy adventure, to make lots of mistakes and learn how not to repeat them!

As Christians, we have the best mirror reflection ever: Jesus!

We can trust God's Word to teach us, guide us, and lead us into a life we are proud of, a life we can hold our head up high, not down because we feel defeated. Do you know how to live like that? You can live as an image-bearer of Christ.

It took many years to see what He sees. He sees that beautiful woman who has battle scars from all of the past battles won. Every time you get knocked down, you are stronger! I know you don't always feel stronger. The fact you are reading this spells *stronger* to me!

The world can be a cruel place, and the enemy doesn't fight fair. Y'all have experienced that for yourself. His ultimate goal is to take you out, but we still win because we get to spend eternity with Jesus.

You look around and see perversion, violence, and hatred. All of what's happening in the world can make you want to hide your face and not leave your home. Stay focused; this isn't it! We have an eternal home.

"But our citizenship is in heaven" (Philippians 3:20, NIV).

My daughter has been known to call me "Woman"! I guess she thinks it is funny. Some name-calling can be funny, but it can also be cruel. What names have you been called? What lies have you believed about who you are? The enemy wants to highlight them and make you believe them. The name-calling, the perversion of the world can all seem larger than the light, love, and joy that Jesus died for us to enjoy. His death settled it all on the cross.

I woke up one morning bright-eyed and bushy-tailed! I was thinking the night before about what it would feel like to actually be on the back of my husband's bike. I mean, to sit close, hold my man, even if I was holding on to a few extra rolls, we are close to our fifties, we have a name for this, Dad bod! LOL.

How many times was this you to awaken with excitement, knowing today was a new day? I will rejoice and be glad in it. Today was going to be my day, the day I conquered my fear. I was going on a bike ride with my husband, I was getting back on the iron horse. I never really fell off of it, but had memories of an ex-boyfriend being wreckless with me on his bike!

I allowed those memories to stop me from getting on my husband's bike. I knew I stalled when I had the chance to ride. I kept telling our teens, "I want your dad to feel comfortable riding his new bike." If he is comfortable and confident riding, then so would I. I mean, it was like a new toy. I wanted my guy to try it out, and then I would join him later. Truth was, I had some hidden fear.

Riding on a motorcycle is the opposite of living in fear. Who even wants to be afraid to do fun things because of that one time someone was reckless? Not me, not anymore! Can you relate to having hidden fears? You were not created to live in bondage. I have an encouraging word for you.

"Don't become so well-adjusted to your culture that you fit into it without even thinking,

Instead, fix your attention on God. You'll be changed from the inside out" (Romans 12:2, MSG).

WONDERFUL SPACES

To find yourself in wonderful spaces, what does that mean to you? What do you spend

your days gazing on? What is wonderful in your life? What

does the word "wonderful" even mean to you? Are you in awe or wonder of anyone or anything? I can tell you; I am in awe of God and His beautiful, wonderful creation to include you and me.

I know wonderful is one of those overused words, kind of like "love"! We love one another in the same breath that we love pizza and chocolate. We love God in the same sentence of loving to exercise. Okay, some of you might not be so in love with exercise, just an example. Here is the million-dollar question! What would you use in the place of love? If you are waiting for me to tell you—Ha! Wrong, I am asking y'all because I don't have the answer. I do know that Jesus is *love*! Love is a noun and a verb. We love because He first loved us. We are loved by God because He created us. Love is also a person, Jesus!

Would you say that your life is wonderful? I am here to tell you it is okay if the answer is

no. You are reading this book because you are on a hunt. Many ways of hunting, men and woman for sure hunt differently! You know how we women like to go down every aisle. What do men do? They go straight for what they want, and they are out! It was a hunt for them.

Life is like a wild hunt. I pray as you read these pages, you discover what you are looking for. If you are like me, you might not even know what that is. I do know what God's Word says about the great hunt. God might not be hunting you, but His love is! We aren't His victims, but the wonder in His eye, the sparkle, the twinkle. We are His great creation.

"I praise you, for I am fearfully and wonderfully made. Wonderful are your works; my soul knows it very well" (Psalm 139:14, ESV).

GUIDING STAR

Grab your backpack, let's go on a hunt for wild joy. It's okay if you're a bit afraid. You are not alone. I am on the journey with you.

If we get lost, Jesus will always be our North Star. A bright light pointing us back to the way home.

I need this reminder daily; God is my North Star, especially during those seasons of feeling lost. Lost isn't just about a destination in your vehicle. Lost can be a way of life. I have many stories of being lost. My daughter was five years old, giving me directions. Thankfully the world was blessed with a GPS. As I head in the wrong direction, "Recalibrating, recalibrating." Can you imagine how that would feel? Jesus singing over you, "Recalibrating"!

The warning signs to get you back on track, to get you on the road He has for you.

All the warning signs in life, who even listens? Shall we look at a young man in the Bible who thought he could run from God? If you grew up in church, this story will resonate with you. If you didn't, turn to the story of Jonah in the book of Jonah (funny story; I didn't know where it was. I asked my daughter where the story of Jonah was, and she said, "I don't know." Then my husband looked it up and shared, to all of our amazement, it is in the book of Jonah). Ha.

Are we serious right now? COVID closed many things down in 2020 to include the church my family helped plant in 2011. The doors closed, and my family watched church online. Oh, how times changed. I personally found a quaint little getaway church I like to sneak away to when I can. The hour drive oh, so worth it. I can tell you I have met some freedom riders in that small congregation. Those people love Jesus and love people. You will hear more about my experiences there.

MESSY TIMES

Messy times, your mess or others mess is when you need some guidance. It is when I need the guiding star, Jesus. You can see the world is a big mess. I am here to remind you that God takes our messes and makes wonderful messages for the world to read.

Men like Jonah, who were running away from God, made a mess. I think we need Bible stories to remember they overcame, and so will you. Thankfully, you don't hear on the news people getting swallowed by a whale because of running from God. Ha.

Even you feel like you missed the mark and messed up beyond no return, God is right there to guide you. His specialty is big messes. If you haven't experienced it already, He loves to make a masterpiece from our mess. Our greatest messes turn into some of our best messages. Your mess might be what someone needs to see. Your mess can be a blessing to someone else. It might show you; you aren't the only one and give you the confidence to make changes. To get out! To give your mess to God! You have to get tired of the mess first.

Being a mom to my Josie Hope has felt like one of my biggest messes! I had so much fear attached to birthing a baby girl. I was afraid because of the lack of relationship I had with my mom. So many questions swirling around like, what do I know about raising a daughter? What am I going to do with a girl? How will I teach her anything about being feminine? I was a tomboy growing up. I raised myself, spending most of my time in the trees, creeks, ponds, and playing in the cornfields. I had adults call me inside to eat, bathe and go to bed, some of my childhood, but I felt like I was on my own most of the time to figure out life.

I don't think my kids will disagree if you asked them, was their childhood fun? I think the whole overcompensating thing kicked in. I wanted to create memories full of love and laughter. I tried to parent from a place of fun and freedom. I shared earlier how I view parenting. I think my husband and I were a good team in how we raised our children. They will more than likely still need therapy. LOL.

Does the smell of the rain bring back good or bad memories? I would say good, and I remember the days of playing in the rain. The rain makes me happy. Freedom and joy envelop me when I am around rain. I don't even have to be out in it; listening to the sound of the rain evokes joy. There is something healing about raindrops falling on my bare skin. It makes me want to spin around and jump in the puddles. I want to twirl around like a little girl who has experienced rain for the first time. I know my daughter loves it, but I don't think my son is too excited about getting his clothes wet or his head, for that matter.

No greater place to feel free, than in the rain. I might be guilty of paying my daughter for a rain experiment. It wasn't too much, only five dollars. All she had to do was stand outside under the big rainy sky. I am so glad she said yes because she was so joyful; no one could wipe that smile off her face. I was really just being silly when I challenged her. Who knew she was going to take me seriously! The gift to my heart was the wild joy I saw in her eyes. She had so much freedom in her movements. She didn't care who saw her or what anyone thought. She took my challenge to heart.

She was free!

She was present in the moment. Something that I have struggled with. I can't say I have totally overcome the moments of caring too much about what others think. My girl reminds me why it doesn't matter. She is my fearless girl. Why I need to care more about what God thinks about me than others.

Wild joy can be found anywhere, even in the rain. Do you feel on the journey to joy? You can find God anywhere. He wants to give you endless opportunities for wild adventures with Him. For real, being a Christian isn't boring. I have found so much fun and excitement in my walk with God.

Being a risk-taker, I try to use cation. When the sky is giving warning signs of danger,

rumbling with thunder, my cue to get my booty inside. God gives you warning signs all day long, and hopefully, the signs move you into safety.

Jesu died for you to live in freedom. I want to be remembered as a freedom rider, no matter if it is playing in the rain, adventures with my children, or hanging on for dear life to my husband. Life is full of wide-open spaces.

Just those memories overwhelm me with feelings of freedom. Another great way to feel free is horseback riding. A good friend of my mom's shared with me on Facebook recently that she and my mom loved to ride her horse. Talk about a joy adventure!

CHAPTER 6:
Puzzle Pieces

God made my life complete when I placed all the pieces before him. When I got my act together, he gave me a fresh start. Now I'm alert to God's ways; I don't take God for granted. Every day I review the ways he works; I try not to miss a trick. I feel put back together, and I'm watching my step. God rewrote the text of my life when I opened the book of my heart to his eyes.

Psalm 18:20-24 (MSG)

My husband and I decided we were going to check out yard sales. These plans were made before we knew the temp in the air would be the fifties. Why was I surprised? Was it October? I was still trying to hold on to the pieces of summer. They were long gone.

Have you ever found yourself trying to hold on to a season too long? I know I have. Maybe you understand not wanting to let go of a season. It might have been as simple as you didn't get all you were looking for. You didn't meet that special someone (yet). You didn't get the dream job or promotion.

Was your head down being busy, and you missed the whole summer working because your boss promised you a promotion if you got that big project done? You are still waiting for that raise. It might be something big like your loved one died unexpectedly. You didn't get to take that trip you saved up for. It is hard to move from one season to the next when you don't feel like you accomplished all that was planned. You didn't get to say goodbye.

Can I ask you, what has been God speaking to you concerning seasons? I know I have learned that I can't wear my flip-flops and tank tops year-round. I live in the south too. Let me rephrase it. I can if I want to, but I am going to suffer and be cold. I do not like being cold. Ask my teenagers; cold makes me grumpy. True story! LOL.

Life can make you want to wear out-of-season clothes. If you know my husband, he wears short pants year-round. I have seen him wear long pants more in the past couple of months than our whole twenty-plus relationship. This guy is no dummy. He puts on pants, thick jeans, or his favorite mustard color cargo pants when he is riding his motorcycle. My guy might not get the wardrobe thing right every time, but he knows about safety and protection. He figured that out quickly; uncovered legs are susceptible to getting burned on hot bike pipes.

Have you ever burned your leg on a hot motor? Me neither, and I want to keep it that way. You won't ever catch me wearing short pants in the winter, especially not on the motorcycle.

Back to the yard sale. My sister's birthday was only a month away, so I was on a search for things to get her—a hunt for anything "owl." I found several little cute owl knick-knacks. I knew she would love the tiny, white salt and pepper shakers. I did wonder about the puzzle I found, sitting all alone. I knew she didn't really like puzzles. But something in me thought, *She might not do puzzles because she has never tried them.* This puzzle was only 500 pieces, unlike the 1000-piece ones I torture myself doing.

I do like a good challenge! I also thought about the great memories we could make. I could see the pieces on her kitchen table. My table was full of my own puzzle pieces. Who knows if she will appreciate the owl puzzle, but what did I have to lose? My heart was in the right place. I wanted to buy her a gift she wouldn't buy herself, and selfishly, I was thinking about a gift that would allow sister quality time.

The whole owl thing is very dear to our hearts. We remembered our mom loved owls. I wish I knew where her love for owls started. I wish I knew why she loved them, but that question, plus a whole long list, stay unanswered. When did she begin to like owls? Did someone buy her a cool owl gift?

What cool, fun, and new thing have you been wanting to try but haven't attempted? Give yourself the opportunity to try it! I also think that you are braver when you have someone to do new things with. Do you have a family member or friend who would join you in your new adventure?

Do I have any Disney fans around me? Tiger is my favorite character, but I wanted to share a quote by Winnie the Pooh. "You're braver than you believe, stronger than you seem, and smarter than you think."

Jesus is always willing to take us on adventures, and, check out this passage, He doesn't judge us; He loves us right where we are.

Jesus answered, "Everyone who drinks this water will be thirsty again, but whoever drinks the water I give them will never thirst. Indeed, the water I give them will become in them a spring of water welling up to eternal life." The woman said to him, "Sir, give me this water so that I won't get thirsty and have to keep coming here to draw water."

John 4:13-15 (NIV)

You can continue on reading the rest. I told you John was my favorite book of the bible. The point I wanted to make was the woman had never been introduced to the real living water; Jesus.

Water is full of play and wonder. It is a place to be a kid. Splash one another playfully and forget about the worries of the day. Are you still enough to feel the moisture in the air? I guess that would mean you're a morning person. Ha. To walk barefoot on the morning dew.

Joy is found in getting your whole self-wet! You might be happy and safe dipping your toes in the water. But you are going to find wild joy, plunging all in, drinking that living water Jesus offers.

The risk of jumping in head first, ready or not! I write a whole chapter on water. Being near water brings me comfort and joy. As I stated before, joy can be found anywhere. Are you seeing a theme here? I find the most joy in being outside and enjoying nature. What places or things bring you comfort? What pieces of life are you missing out on?

FUN EXERCISE

You may be wondering how do you discover the puzzle pieces of your life? How do you move forward and not let fear hold you back anymore? You move forward by starting. Have you started? What do you like? What brings your heart joy? Who and how did God make you? Have you taken the time to get to know yourself?

I have a very good friend who will, any time of the day, say yes to joining me in fun tests. We like to find tests that help us better understand our personality traits. We spent hours taking the different tests and then emailing them to each other because she lived in another state. I recently found the results of our Myer Briggs personality test.

As I was reading the email, I was reminded it was a silly test, yes, but God is the one who reveals my identity, not an online test. If you decide to dive into these tests, study the root, origin, and history of where they come from. God has a plan and purpose for your life, and only He can fully reveal it.

I also am a big fan and believer of the "5 Love Languages" quiz. I guess it is a test too, but I am calling it a quiz because you will be quizzed on the way you show love. It is a game-changer! If you don't know what I am talking about, I highly challenge/encourage you to take the life-revealing test already! You can even take it online.

You are very welcome. Everyone in your house will be thanking me. LOL. I made sure my whole family took the quiz because we are a military family, and Tim has deployed a lot. I wanted to be armed with connections in my family. As you might have guessed, I ranked high on "words of affirmation." There are five different love languages. The second one I scored high on was "receiving gifts."

I am very honored and humbled to have you reading these pages. I know God showed me years ago, writing would help get me through some of the darkest days of my life. I had no idea then what God would do and that I would feel the calling to write books. I am still blown away by God's goodness.

I can hear some of you now, "What is the point?" The point is life is too short not to know who God made you to be. I also want to tell you in my "mom voice" (loud) it is never too late to start! The best time to start is now, honey child! I'm sure my family got tired of me quoting, "The best time to do anything is now! When is the best time to do something? Now!"

This book was born from my believing this, not just saying it; the best time is *now*! Y'all, if I would have waited until the perfect time, you would not be reading these pages. That is

why chapter one starts out with my "why" and a verse about being present. When you are present, then you are aware, alive, and awakened to hearing from God.

I actually had a dream about Dr. Gary Chapman. I told you God speaks to me in my dreams. He asked me of all people to work his book table. Me! It was like we were old friends. We were at this event together, and he was promoting his books. I saw him in my dream and immediately knew who he was! I said, "You are the guy who wrote the book with a heart on the cover. It was so cool. I have been a believer in the love languages for years."

The dream prompted me to go find my own copy of *5 Love Languages*. I found it and began to read it. The time was right on because my husband left a month later for a business trip. I needed all the reminders of how to stay connected when his top two were acts of service and quality time.

My first piece to discover in being a writer was cultivating the habit of journaling. I was

a young girl when I started expressing my thoughts on paper. I had no clue what God was doing.

I just knew I felt so much better after I journaled. If this is a new concept to you, no worries! You simply start with documentation of your thoughts.

Our thoughts can be cloudy or jumbled. God wants you to make room for the spaces to

create, build, and dream. I like to call journaling a "brain dump." You can tend to allow negative thinking, better known as stinking thinking, to take up free space in your minds. Why spend one more second focusing on your weaknesses?

How about taking the time to identify your strengths? Jesus died for you to live in your strengths. Those superhero powers He gave you are to be used, not saved for a rainy day. Every day is a good day to live in your power. To live in the power of Jesus.

Let me ask you a question, where has all the negativity got you in life? I am offering you

a new piece to your puzzle of life. In this new season, God is saying, "I want to help you focus on your strengths." What are a few things you like about yourself?

Another fun exercise. Think of three to five attributes you like about yourself. I really want you to take this seriously. I'll even wait for you. Let's take a few minutes and write those things down. This exercise is really important. Believe me, I know it's easier to pick the things you don't like about yourself.

I want to remind you; life isn't about easy. Self-discovery isn't a cakewalk. Tapping into that wild joy means you are willing to go places you haven't gone before; remember to have things you have never had. You are not alone. God is guiding you.

REAL YOU

One of the most rewarding parts of this journey will be introducing you to the real you. I

can tell you from experience; once you accept yourself, then you'll be able to accept others. This

will create a life of freedom. I'm not going to ask you to do anything I haven't already done. Keep in mind I've been doing this exercise for many years. Please don't compare. You're just getting started with where I am right now!

I, for one, need a daily reminder not to compare myself to others. I know it can look like others are farther along than you. In the game of comparison, nobody wins. In God's economy, we are all winners. You are a winner!

I like to encourage others. Sending cards and texts are one of my favorite ways to do that. I also like that I am kind. If you ever sent me a gift, then you more than likely got a personal handwritten thank you card from me. I started realizing in my older years that when someone gave me a gift, if I didn't send them a card, it didn't mean I didn't appreciate it. I used to feel so guilty and think that the other person didn't know how much I liked their gift. See how fast I went from; I like to encourage to what made me feel guilty. I know our minds can play tricks. Those tricks can trip you up!

You are reading this book because you are in a growing season. I am in a growing season too! Allowing myself to receive has been an ongoing lesson. Gifting giving is more my thing, but a healthy balance is to give and receive. I can see now the gift-giving really matters because it is one way I express my love. I am so thankful for the ultimate gift, Jesus.

God's truth always shines light on the lies. I was believing a lie; if I didn't send a thank you card, then that meant I wasn't thankful for the gifts I received. I really worked on allowing myself to receive without having to do anything in return, just a simple thank you in person or in text. I am grateful for the truth. The years of therapy were showing me why I did the things I did. Why I made certain choices in my life, all of those choices led me right here, right here with all of you.

God's ultimate plan is for you to be the healthiest version of yourself. You know what that involves, taking responsibility for the choices that paved the path for your life.

God has been showing you pieces of your life. I personally don't think we will complete

the whole puzzle on this earth. Our life story isn't over until we enter into our eternal home, heaven. There you get to start all over without any sickness or disease. All of those questions won't even matter; you won't have pain or problems. It will be so glorious.

To be honest, I have a lot of peace believing this: when we get to the pearly gates, we

are going to be so thrilled that we made it; all that other stuff just isn't going to matter!

It helps me to put things into perspective. That eagle view, to live with a heavenly perspective means you live above the storms of life.

Stop for a few seconds, think about some areas of your life that you need to ask yourself, how much does this really matter? Will this matter in one year, five years, or ten years? Do what I call housecleaning—the housecleaning of your heart, of your mind.

I can't finish this chapter without sharing a big puzzle piece. It took me twenty years to gain this revelation, but hey, better late than never, right!

For now, I want to share how Mr. Joy was introduced to me. A military man turned husband. Most people would not look at Tim and think joy! Ha! Not this guy because he might be known to have some walls up and be a bit rough around the edges. But Tim has taught me so much about love, joy, and hope.

He has shown me unconditional love. He has been an awesome father and husband. Joy isn't always about happy-go-lucky all the time. Remember, joy is deeper; it is a jewel. Joy is a rare commodity. My husband describes all that and more!

Tim carries confidence, an inner strength, a renewed hope that good men do exist. He has shown me so much grace, support, encouragement over the past twenty years. I am blessed to be his wife. Some relationships aren't for keeps, but I know this one is. I am married to my friend, Mr. Joy. It still feels silly to say that, but I really do believe it. Joy causes you to laugh, and believe me, I laugh a lot around him, and joy can evoke tears. I also expel my share my tears with him.

I have heard people come into your life for many reasons and certain seasons. Some stay and some go, some you will be glad didn't stay, and some you will be sad to see leave. I can't help but share a favorite scripture.

"There is a time for everything, and a season for every activity under the heavens" (Ecclesiastes 3:1, NIV).

God had plans for my life that I couldn't even see. Not only did He bring a man into my

life who would exude joy, but He also took me on my own joy journey. Trying the whole

marriage thing for the second time was a wild ride. If you have ever gone through a divorce,

you know the feeling of being a failure no matter the circumstances or who asked for it. I had to

trust God this time would be different.

You might not be able to relate if you've never been married. Hopefully, many of you haven't gone through a divorce. It is hard, and you are not a bad person if you did. God loves you just the same. You have your own story of trusting God one more time. I am reminded of another person who exuded joy. He was a stranger turned friend quickly. This guy is a retired military man who now spends his days blessing children with special needs. He wears a red jacket and black boots. Many know this jolly man as a Santa. Do y'all think he saw himself as a professional Santa during those military days?

But God...

He trusted God one more time with his life. My husband and I were very grateful to meet this retired man. A great reminder not to tell God what you won't do! The timing was perfect when we met him because retirement was knocking on Tim's door. You don't always know what is in your future.

How boring would that be if we could predict everything that was going to happen in our lives? Boring, if you ask me! Now I struggle at times with getting a bit worried about what life

looks like when my husband and I are empty nesters. Then I have to remind myself I am not in control.

There are pieces of the puzzle you have to trust God to bring. I am more excited and

hopeful about my future than ever before. I wish I could share a formula with you, but I told you

at the beginning of this book, no cookie-cutter solutions here.

I began to trust God more than I ever! That might be surprising to some of you, and some of you might be in a season where you feel the same way. The bottom line is I know who holds the future, God! I just have to be willing to let go and let God hold my future. I really don't think He needs my help, or does He? LOL. I am just kidding. Seriously, how many times do we try to help God? "Hey God, I have a puzzle piece over here you missed!" In those moments, I am not trusting God but leaning on what I think is best and what puzzle pieces I think will fit.

CHAPTER 7:
That Girl

Whatever I have, wherever I am, I can make it through anything in the One who makes me who I am.

Philippians 4:13 (MSG)

The verse above isn't just words; they are lifelines to what kept me afloat in darker days of my life. Philippians is the first book of the Bible I memorized. I don't know all the verses, but I have hidden enough of them in my heart to change my heart. In the year 1990, I found myself married and then divorced. I made so many mistakes during that time. What I can be proud of is May 1992, the year I graduated high school.

Do you have a year that is highlighted in your own life? That year helped to guide the way and pave the path for "that girl." I hope this chapter helps you to form your own, that girl.

Ready. Set. Go!

I Miss You

I miss my dad so much.

My heart misses his love.

I miss his hugs.

I miss his laughter.

I miss my dad so much.

My heart hurts for what won't be.

I want him back.

I want him here.

My heart is crying tears.

I can't believe my dad isn't near.

One day I will see him whole.

I will see a smile on his face.

No tears, only love will remain.

Until then, my heart feels pain.

Joannie Garner *(39 days after my dad's death)*

"I can do all this through him who gives me strength" (Philippians 4:13, NIV).

First, you need to know this about me. I am not the girl who thinks she isn't enough. I am that girl who has thought of her life, *I am too much. Others are going to tire of me and leave me like my mom and dad did.*

I am loud, I am passionate, I am silly, and I am full of energy. I love to travel to new places and meet new people. I also like to explore new places and visit familiar places. I love vibrant and neon colors. I have my own hippie style and crazy patterns. My sister will tell you, I don't always match, but my goal isn't to fit in with the rest of the world. Why wear white when you can wear hot pink? Why wear black when you can wear zebra or cheetah print?

Remember, I am the girl who lives life to the fullest because what is the point of living? I know what it feels like to be stuck in survival mode. I know how it feels to be on a hamster wheel. I know how it feels to be drowning. I am that girl who hit a brick wall and landed in a

therapist's office sitting on a plaid couch. I learned the brick wall was me.

I am that girl who used to be afraid of the dark, even of my own shadow at times. I am the girl who had too many nightmares that left her afraid to go to sleep. I am the girl who was left to wonder who was going to tell her "goodnight" with hugs and kisses to make her feel safe. I am the girl who was left at home to care for my siblings while my mom went to bars.

I am also that girl who used to look out of the window and wait for her dad to come home. It seemed hours would pass, and so many tears shed. I am that girl who was hoping to see him walking or driving down the street. I spent many days wondering what was wrong with me and why didn't he want me. Why wasn't I loveable enough for him to stay? Why did he leave my family? Why did he leave me?

I am the girl who spends her days in the clouds, dreaming of a better tomorrow. I am that girl who has visions and is crazy enough to believe they will happen. See them happen. I am the girl who has vivid dreams and believes God is speaking. I am the girl who always has a journal close by.

I am the girl who grew up not feeling wanted and got wrapped up in people-pleasing so I

wouldn't be left alone. I thought if I disagreed with you, then you wouldn't like me, and I would

be left without any friends.

I am the girl who fears what others think of her. I am that girl who is known to lose sleep or obsessed a little too much over someone not liking her.

I am the girl who didn't read books in her childhood and now reads all the time. And now I am that girl who is going after her dream and publishing her first book, with more to come.

I am the girl who loves to eat, better known as a foodie. I am the girl who could be eating sushi, tacos, fresh veggies, or drinking kombucha on any given day. Let's not forget all types of fruit, especially berries. I am that girl with an appetite not only for food but spiritual food.

I am that girl who doesn't understand herself at times but knows God understands me. I am that girl with a hunger for more and an insatiable thirst for the truth—the girl who has a hard time staying full.

Let's be honest, that girl who struggles with her addictions daily.

THE GIRL

The girl who loves Jesus. The girl who grew up in a broken home with a broken heart. But, God. That girl who loves deep but grieves deeper. The girl who has been known to put her hands over her face to hide her tears.

The girl who lost herself every time a loved one died. The girl who seemed to have it all

together but, on the inside, was slowly dying.

The girl who battled demons nobody could see. The girl who was left alone to try to understand an aching in her heart.

The girl who stays up way too late, a night owl. The girl who was spontaneous, who loves surprises, and sitting in the sunshine. The girl who found solace sitting in her bed, looking out her window.

The girl who finds more fulfillment in being a mom and wife more than any career or success the world had to offer.

The girl who never gives up on her dream of being an author. Proof! You are reading these words. Let this give you power and courage to never give up on your own dreams.

The girl who stood by her military husband and loved him more than she ever knew was possible. That girl who loved and cared for his mother, who became like her own mother.

The girl who is the life of the party and not afraid to take risks. She might even teach you some of her dance moves!

The girl who gave until she had nothing left to give. The girl who got sick and tired of her life and sought out counseling.

The girl who continued to grow like the wild lilies in a field.

The girl who knows she had to be a friend to have a friend.

The girl who lived out her truth and helps others do the same.

The girl who obeyed the laws but lived to make up her own rules. She didn't like being told what to do or how to do it (don't even ask how she made it six years in the military!).

That girl who questioned her worth and value but knew God was the only one who could define her. He was the one who gave her purpose.

The girl who still struggles with being too much and trying to overcompensate in all areas of her life. The girl who was attached to things and let things clutter her head home.

The girl who loves to empower women! The girl who lives for the opportunity to share truth and remind women who God made them to be.

The girl who is obsessed with Elvis and *Wonder Woman*.

There you go, my readers. Now you know more about me. Your turn, take the time to write your list and then share it with someone.

A new way to discover wild joy for yourself and to help others. What a fun but exhausting at times on this wild and beautiful ride called life. I pray you not only discover wild joy but the wild love of God.

DIGGING DEEPER

Wild joy can be found anywhere. I found it in the wilderness, valleys, and on the mountaintops. It's a precious gem that needs to be excavated out of dark places. It shines the brightest in the light. How is gold formed and found? You have to dig past the bedrock layer to get to the gold.

All women like diamonds, right? Men love to buy women diamonds, right! LOL. Did you know how diamonds are formed? Diamonds are formed out of coal under immense pressure. Can I get an "amen" on feeling covered up with dirt, waiting to be found as you are under all that pressure? Gold and diamonds are some of the most precious materials on this earth. Do you really think they were just lying on top of the ground waiting to be discovered? No! They were not discovered on top of the ground but under all that dirt.

Only God could turn a piece of coal into a beautiful diamond, every woman's best friend! If you are married and have a wedding ring on, take a minute to look at your diamond. Just take this minute to enjoy the beauty and the shine. You wouldn't be wearing that diamond if someone didn't do the deep digging to find it. The process of being found, being discovered took endless hours of deep digging.

Why do we think we don't have to do the deep digging work? Are you ready to do the deep digging in your life? The shallow places aren't going to get it anymore. God has created you to be a beautiful warrior. I will share more about that.

"They are more precious than gold, than much pure gold"
(Psalm 19:10, NIV).

This is how I found wild joy, digging deeper into the layers of my life. You might get dirty, but who cares! You might even get a few calluses and scars, but guess what? They are there to remind you it was worth it! I'm not going to promise it's easy, but it'll be worth it. Your face will be covered in smudges, and you might even be left with a few cuts and bruises. At times, you will find yourself in small spaces. You might even wonder how you fit in those spaces. Then the question of how do you get out.

I feel like that slogan, "Diamonds are a girl's best friend," needs to be, "Diamonds were created for God's girls because they were created from the dirt."

"God's Word is better than a diamond, better than a diamond

set between emeralds" (Psalm 19:10, MSG).

I want to reassure you; I am cheering you on. You will get to the other end! You can't see it now, but the other side is glorious. It will be worth every ounce of energy you invest and energy you deplete. Are you ready? The preparation has begun. I am confident we will get through this together with Jesus as our compass. He will direct the path if you let Him. Wild joy is discovered in wild, weird, and wonderful places.

My deepest digging started after my dad died. I had no clue the hidden fear I had attached to death. I didn't have a healthy perspective of death. I lost my mom at such a young age, and there was so much controversy around suicide. Part of my survival was not to think about it. I knew deep down in my heart, one day, I would see my mom again.

The days after my dad's death would be some of my darkest days. Please don't think someone has to die in order to find wild joy. More than likely, you have your own stories of death. You might even be in that season now. No one is immune to loved ones dying.

What a lesson I didn't know I needed. Death is part of the cycle of life, and with God on your side, you don't have to be afraid. Please don't wait until you are in your forties to look death in the face and tell it that you aren't afraid anymore! I was so scared but so full of sorrow. I didn't care anymore, I didn't have anything to lose, I just lost my person. I was mad at life! I wanted someone to pay for my pain. I was so tired of being punked and bullied by the enemy

The day I looked death in the eyes is the day I truly became free. Free to feel, free to deal, free to really heal, free to live the way I was created to live. To live by faith not by fear.

Everyone knows how to smile. It's one of the greatest gifts God has given us. A smile makes people feel good, and people look so beautiful when they smile. When the joy in your life is obvious, it rubs off on others.

Wild Joy

Our smile is a gift we can offer others. The only thing a smile might cost you is your pride. To suck it up and remember why you are grateful.

Writing this book taught me I couldn't do it alone. The "it" takes on so many nouns and verbs. Shall we discuss one "it" at a time? The "it" I am referring to is death. Have you faced death? Have you thought about where your loved ones who passed are? Have you lost someone you loved so much that you thought your heart was breaking into tiny pieces?

Some of you may have hurt so deep that you're done trusting others. I get that, and I have been there. I could write a whole book on trust and still have a lifetime to learn more. All I know is one person who deserves my full trust, and His name is Jesus! I even struggle at times, trusting Jesus. But God....

Wild joy is not found living on an island. Your pain, your past, and your present make up the sum total of your life. The people you have met. Your family you were born in. The friends you choose to do life with. Think about your school days, your first job, your college experience,

your co-workers at your job now. The people you went to church and might currently still do life

with. Yes, all of these people are what I am talking about. We make memories, we share life, we

swap stories, and we discover wild joy.

Many people get stuck in the past. Getting stuck happens because of the unanswered questions. How many times have we asked the three simple letters, "Why?" This is what I mean. Why did my mom have to die? Why was I not worth fighting for? Why could I not stop her from taking her own life? Why was I only twelve years old? Why didn't I have more time with her? Why was I spared from witnessing the abuse the last night of her life, but my siblings weren't? Why did she have to drink so much? Why did my dad have to go away? Why did my dad have an affair with her best friend? Why did he think my siblings and I needed a mom a month after her death? Why did my dad die in his sixties? Why, why, and why some more!

The lingering questions of *why* haunt us, torment us, teach us until we discover who we are and whose we are. God isn't going to be mad at you for asking all the why questions. I want you to know that we won't have all the answers, and it is okay. If you aren't feeling okay, then be reassured you will be okay one day.

I read a book a friend sent to me after my dad died. The whole message gives you permission to be okay to not be okay. I highly recommend *It's Okay Not to Be Okay* by Shelia Walsh.

YOUR NAME MATTERS

I want to share a recent revelation I had about my name. As a little girl, as a teenager, and as an adult, I always wondered why my parents spelled my name the way they did. Another one of those haunting "why" questions. I told you, I have many of my own to figure out. I wanted my

name to be spelled "Joni." Just a simple four-letter name, I could spell easily, and others wouldn't butcher or pronounce it wrong. I knew I was named after my grandmother Joan.

My name being spelled "Joan," I get, but I didn't get the "nnie" part, especially the "nn" part. I wanted to be able to find my name on keychains. I never ever heard of anyone spelling their name like mine. It hit me one day in a deep conversation with a sweet, sweet lady who would be like a spiritual mom to me. She sent me an email addressing how she spelled my name wrong. I was blessed to spend the whole afternoon with her. She said, "I am going to add the other "n" to your name." LOL.

In my response to her, I said, "Okay, no worries, many people misspell my name." I do appreciate it. Then it was like the Lord was speaking to me. He said, "I named you Joannie. I am the one who was responsible for naming you. Do you really think I created you to live with one 'n'? Your personality is too big for one 'n,'

I gave you two n's on purpose. You even said to yourself, Joannie, with two n (s). You are a bit 'extra,' and extra people don't have just one 'n' in their name!" Ha.

God really set me straight, and you know He was right! I promise I am not trying to say I am any better than anyone else. I want to let you know that the Lord named you, and He loves you. He might not be calling you "extra," but He might be trying to get your attention about other things.

He thinks you are special.

He loves you. He sees you.

He thought about your name before your mom even had you.

FRIENDSHIPS

Have you ever had those friends in your life who got a little too close for your comfort? Yes, me too! When this happens, you are at a crossroads to move closer or move away. If you move away, you might be missing one of the greatest friendships! I found these crossroads are about drawing you closer to intimacy, an invitation to grow, a deeper heart connection.

Intimacy is into you, I see.

If you haven't experienced this, then get ready because you are about to. An invitation, an up-close and personal call to a deeper connection. Will you answer the call?

Friendships are like shoes. We have our favorite pairs, the ones that are comfortable, the ones that really fit, and the ones we have outgrown. If you keep those shoes that no longer fit, do you find yourself trying to put them on and squeeze your foot in them?

The shoes that are in my closet vary, and I am sure yours do too! I have combat boots, and they remind me of those friends who will go to battle with me. You can call or text them anytime to pray for you. The friends you find yourself in the trenches of life with, your muddy-faced friends. The ones who belly crawl with you to get help others. We all need a helping hand from time to time.

I also have my high-heel friends. They are the ones you get dressed up and go to dinner with or out dancing. This time in my life, it's more about the low heel shoes. But I do believe the high-heel friends will throw one of their shoes for you if the occasion calls for it. They might even break a heel. LOL.

Then you have your flip-flop friends. They are the ones who you hang out with, and the time together feels effortless. They are carefree, and it doesn't matter how long you have gone without talking. When you see each other, it is like no time has passed between the two of you. You have fun with these friends and enjoy the simple things in life.

Let's not forget our tennis shoes. These are what I wear when I am working out, walking, running errands, basically getting things done. They are comfortable and made for all types of activity. I love these friends who are healthy and full of endurance because they are my running buddies. They are the ones who are running towards the finish line. Now, I do want to say some of your friends can fit all the shoes. Who am I to say? It is your life and your friendships. I can only share my friendships experiences and this revelation of friendship.

I know there are so many more kinds of shoes, but those are the types that best fit the friends in my life. I don't even have enough time or pages to share with you the wonderful friends God has blessed me with. Riches aren't just about silver or gold but the rich relationships in your life.

I have learned the hard way to hold my friends lightly. Some are for seasons and will not be with you for the long haul. It is wise to learn what God wants you to learn and let them go. Holding on too tightly is painful when they leave your life. Some friends are not for the long haul. I have shed many tears over friends I thought would be what some people refer to as lifers. You do not have control over who stays in your life. God is the one ultimately in control and gives you freedom in choosing people to do life with.

Friendships are worth fighting for. I encourage you to allow yourself to move closer to those you feel God wants you to share life with. I try every year to ask God, "Who do you want me to invest in this year?" Friendships involve an investment of your time, emotional and mental. Don't give up too quickly on those people who you feel are afraid to get too close. Like I mentioned, friendships are worth the investment and energy to stay in a relationship.

Your family can be some of the hardest ones to spend time with. Have you ever thought because you are so much like them? I know it feels like a mirror sometimes when doing life with your family. We don't always want to see the things that aren't so pleasant in others because it makes us stop and think about those attributes in ourselves.

We are all afraid of something. That something might be intimacy for you, and that is okay. I know God is calling you closer to Him. I shared with you many things I am scared of. When you open your heart to God, He can and will take you further than you ever imagined.

To keep fighting is to not give up. To keep loving is to be like Jesus.

I encountered a season where I could feel my heart growing a bit bitter and offensive. I was starting to pull away from people. Y'all, I am an extra, extra extrovert, so I need people in my life. See, that is what makes me feel uncomfortable; the needing anyone part. But I do like

sharing life with others. I like daily visits and conversations. I like to know that someone has my

back and accepts me just the way I am. I love to process out loud as I share my feelings. I think you get the point. What was I doing pulling away? I was afraid for others to see my pain, to see my weakness, to see my vulnerability. I was a fragile mess.

You are reading these words, which means that season didn't take me out. It pushed me closer to God. The drawing close to God eventually led me closer to my friends. Those friends who were watching me go into my hole. It was a form of self-preservation. I was trying to protect myself.

Are you evaluating your shoes and friendship now? Good! When have you been isolated because you wanted to protect yourself from any more pain? Or who is going through it as you read these words? I talked about being "that girl," what would your "that girl" or "that guy" story sound like? Write the book, start journaling, be a friend to have a friend, stay open to what God is doing in your life. He will guide you as you dig deeper.

CHAPTER 8:
Identity Theft

*The thief comes only to steal and kill and destroy; I have come
that they may have life, and have it to the full.*

John 10:10 (NIV)

Another top favorite verse. It comes in close running with
John 8:32. I guess I can admit, the book of John is the winner of
the books of the Bible. I do love the Word of God, but this book
has got me through some really rough patches. If you are reading
this, then you are alive, and that means you have gone through
good and bad times. This verse brings me back to reality when I
feel like my head and life are spinning out of control.

I want to point you back to Jesus. The one who came to save
you. The one who died for you to live the abundant lifestyle. The
one who gets you. The one who knows a thing or two about having a life being stolen from and destroyed.

Well, His Spirit wasn't destroyed, Jesus rose up after being
crucified, but He first died a

gruesome death for you.

I didn't know where to put this title; I even struggled with the
name. At first, I thought it was an identity crisis, but one day, soak-
ing in the tub, praying all my worries away, I felt the Lord give
me the word "theft." I knew God wanted to heal my heart. I even
asked my husband what he thought about the word. Instead of giving you the Webster definition. Here is Tim Garner's definition:

Identity crisis: when you don't know who you are.

Identity theft: when someone steals who you are.

I can relate to both of those. What about yourself?

I want to break these down a bit. When you don't know who you are, you are left in this world to be anyone. You can take on another person's identity, and that is what people do every day. Have you ever met someone and thought something seems off about that person? They didn't seem like themselves. This could happen with strangers or people you know. You might even see changes start to happen in others that make them unrecognizable.

When I look in the mirror now, I don't even recognize the lost, scared little girl I once was. I see an adult woman who has aged lines, grey hair, and a smile on her face. I see a woman full of joy. I can see sadness in the depth of her eyes because I am her. I know where she has been. I know the loss she has encountered. I know the battles she has won.

The years of counseling, life skills, Bible studies, and therapy have paid off! I once was

disconnected from that fearful little girl. Now I am not afraid of her, and she isn't afraid of me. I

loved her back to life. She was a little warrior who wanted to feel safe. She wanted to know why

she existed and see the world as a safe place. I won't even lie, I still get afraid, but my core, my being, the little warrior, and the big warrior are one. They are connected because God

created them both.

"Therefore, if anyone is in Christ, the new creation has come: The old has gone, the new is here!" (2 Corinthians 5:17, NIV).

I thought I knew what these two words meant, "self-discovery."

Until I didn't! Until I was so undone, I didn't know much of anything.

I forgot who I was and where I belonged. I found myself in an identity crisis. It didn't

happen overnight. I didn't wake up one morning. It was a slow decline of who I was. Who God

made me and why God made me. I was unsure of my purpose. The thing is, if you looked at my

life, you would see a smile. No one knew the real story behind that smile. I let others see who I wanted them to see. I wasn't even able to be the real me because I lost sight of who that person was.

The day that I lost my person, my dad, was the day a new life was birth. I stumbled upon a newfound space. I no longer had the man who helped bring me into this world, my dad. No warning signs, no preparation, no nothing but a phone call that would change the trajectory of my life. As I write this, it was only seven months ago. In my naive mind, I thought my book was already written. I also thought I had more time with my dad. I thought I would get to share the healthier parts of me with him. I thought he would see my teens get married. I thought he would meet his new grandchildren. I thought, I thought, and I thought until I thought no more.

No more dreams of sharing a brighter tomorrow with my dad. No more planned visits.

No more surprise phone calls. No more silly Facebook posts and comments. No more of my dad saying, "You know I love you, baby."

A SPACE OF DISCOVERY

Wild joy is not a location or a destination; it is a space to be discovered. A discovery of

self, God, and others. At least this has been my experience. I can't wait until you trip upon

your own wild joy journey! I will warn you; you might find yourself in the wilderness. Don't be alarmed. The wilderness is where I felt the most alive.

Y'all, if you're looking for a good ole perfect Christian girl, then you're holding the

wrong book, and you got the wrong girl. I see you! My beautiful joy-seeking reader. Thank you for giving this sister a chance and for buying my book. I am far, far, far from perfect. Just an imperfectly blessed, Jesus girl who loves life to the fullest.

Each year, I start off with a fresh new focus, a new word. In the year 2020, I "needed my new word." Some years, the words are a bit strange and unfamiliar like, "awaken" or "bliss." Most years, they are simple and familiar like "joy" and "free."

The quarantine year, 2020, was "discover." The word "discover" can mean so many things to so many people. A theme I noticed, most of my words the past eight years have been about action. A verb! To move forward! To get unstuck! To learn more about the depth of God's love.

I wanted to dive deeper into who God made me. You would think I would know a small bit about myself at a ripe age forty-five years old. Wrong! I'm still searching for the real Joannie. My prayer, as I share you learn more about yourself.

I also wanted to learn more about my mom. To learn more about her pain and the

darkness of suicide. I knew there had to be more to her life. She was a divorced and single

woman, raising four children.

Part of my mojo to finish this book, my parents were with Jesus cheering me on. They were without pain in Heaven awaiting my arrival. I had this cool vision of my dad and God planning something big for me. They both know me so well and what is best for my life, especially God. Writing, writing, and writing these pages were a good healthy distraction to not sit in the pain, the loss, the heartbreak of my dad being gone. I needed something bigger than myself to work on, to know I was still being used by

God.

Every time I see a male cardinal, I can feel the spirit of my dad. My life felt like a

deep void; a piece of me was missing. The cardinal brings me joy. I see it as a God wink.

I no longer had to struggle with, "Does he love me? Does he love me not? Why doesn't he come to see me? Why doesn't he want to visit his grandchildren? I saw on Facebook the times he visited his other daughters, but why not me?" I knew that their relationship was different than mine, but it didn't lessen the sting.

All that wasted energy, I didn't want to make the same mistakes. At times, the negative thoughts haunted me. I know a girl will always want her dad's love. It totally heals my heart to see the attention and time my husband gives our daughter. The fondness and love he has for her melts me. I watch their special bond and would never want to do anything to change that. I love they connect in a deep way. Josie will always be her daddy girl.

My eyes were open to a whole new world. I lived in an unfamiliar grief. A space I wasn't sure day to day how to maneuver. Again, my writing saved me! I poured my heart and time into this manual. As I read the pages I already wrote, lots of headspaces were shared, but where were the stories shared from the heart? It seemed I had more to learn and share.

You would think my dad's death would have close me off, but in actuality, it opened up a new way to write. I was in a season of refinement. God was doing refining; He was burning up those places that no longer served me well.

What I didn't want to do was sound so proper and polished; you couldn't relate. I am not

saying I wanted to have a bunch of grammatical errors. That is why I paid a publishing company

to clean it up! That cleaning up was also happening in my everyday waking life.

I found myself sorting through everything I did. I started asking myself more questions. Do you know what happened? My curiosity started to blossom. I seemed to be less stuck by those why questions around my mom's death and my dad's love. I started to reframe my thoughts, and my questions changed. Why didn't my dad love me? I knew my dad loved me. Why did it take me so long to believe in my dad's love?

I want to pause there for a minute with you. Can you relate?

How does this make you feel about your relationship with God?

You are around the halfway mark. Keep reading! I know I still have healing when it

comes to my parents. My hope would be I could forgive them more for the things I didn't understand, for the conversations I never had with them, for them not being the parents I thought they needed to be. I had to let go of the judgment, the expectations of what I thought.

Have you ever worked on a project and knew something was missing, but you didn't know what? I wonder, really ponder, would I have gotten this deeper healing without writing my manual. If I would have continued to write from a safe place and not open up my heart. Would I be living in the healing from their deaths? What is the family picture I found during editing, I would have packed away because of the hurt?

What if I didn't choose to place it next to my computer? Would I? Would you get the healing you are desiring without digger deeper into parts of yourself and God you might have closed off?

Perfectionism can, for sure, steal from you! I used to struggle with all the mistakes I made. "I must not be smart," "How dare I make a mistake?" "Don't I know better?" All the trash-talking had to stop. I will also let you in on a little secret; I am a recovering people-pleaser.

If you sat down with my dear husband, he would tell you. I may have had a wee bit of anger issues. He might even describe it as someone going from zero to a hundred in half a second. I know the anger was from years and years of unresolved hurt and pain. Wounds that were not visible to the eye but scars on my heart. Again, this is who I once was. My anger and unresolved pain hijacked my identity.

To lose something valuable.

To be mugged.

To be taken advantage of.

To feel lost.

To have something stolen.

To feel worthless.

The other desire for this path of discovery is about others. That would include you! The curiosity about how habits are formed and how addictions are started. Why do we do what we do? How can a mom of four leave her children behind? How can a woman give her babies up for adoption? How can a woman go through an abortion and make it out alive? How? How? You fill in the blanks with your personal story.

I really wish I was sitting next to you with a cup of hot tea, warm in my hands as you go deeper into this book. Some of you might be sippin' on a glass of wine. No matter your drink of choice, I am picturing you holding my book, reading the pages with eyes wide open to learn more about yourself as you hear my story.

My prayer for you is that you get to know the real you. If we were together, you might see me standing on a rooftop, yelling, "This is where real freedom comes from!" Being introduced to the real you. Since we are not together, I want to encourage you with these words. If you were sitting at my house, the first thing I would do is offer you bottled water. This seems to be the next best thing, or really the best thing, since God's Word is the bread of life.

"The Lord will guide you always; he will satisfy your needs in a sun-scorched land and will strengthen your frame. You will be like a well-watered garden" (Isaiah 58:11, NIV).

Remember, I am that girl who has many favorite verses. But I do, I beg of you to find your own. If you already have one, then I am so proud! If you do not have one, then I am still proud as you search for your own favorite verse. Philippians 4:13 was the first verse, and it was a lifesaver! I found myself not only married in the '90s but also divorced. I told y'all, I am imperfectly blessed! This verse isn't just words but a precious gift that God used to save me.

There were many not-so-great choices in my early and later years. This should be no surprise with a girl who was looking for love in all the wrong places. I also thought a great life choice would be to join the military. Don't worry! You will hear more about my Boot Camp experience later. I don't regret any of my decisions, but I would not recommend them, especially to my lovely teenagers. They will have to make their own choices. After all, isn't that what we all want in life? To have the freedom to make our own choices and then take our own path. Stumbling and falling flat on your face but being aware! To know your true identity, God comes from God. To recognize when you are a victim of identity theft. To take your life back!

CHAPTER 9:
Splish Splash

It is life, I think, to watch the water. A man can learn so many things.

Nicholas Sparks

Taking hot baths is one of my favorite pastimes. Like for real, I have been known to stay in the tub for hours. If you add a good book, then you could find me sitting in a bathtub without water. I am not even joking, not sure if that is a good thing or a bad thing. The hot water calms me; it warms my soul. I feel safe in water.

I feel safe and wrapped up in God's love.

The water has always been healing to my soul. One of the tools that helped me tremendously during different seasons of grief was my red-hot water bottle. You can find it at your local drugstore. I am sure you could order it online. This water bottle has been a lifesaver! My old-school rusty orange whistling pot, I mean screaming tea kettles, is sitting on my stove, always ready to be filled up for a cup of tea or to pour into the rubber water bottle.

Something about seeing that kettle brings me comfort and reminds me I'm at home no matter what is going on in my life. My daughter Josie had to order her own because we would fight over mine once she hit that real puberty age. She would say, "Mom, can you please bring me the 'red thing.'" I knew exactly what she was talking about, especially by the tone of her voice. She enjoyed the heat most when dealing with menstrual cramps. She found her own comfort with the rubber bottle. She ended up putting her initial on hers, so we didn't get them mixed up. She said hers worked better; I think mine had a leak due to much usage. LOL.

After my dad died, I spent many nights falling asleep, almost snuggling against my rubber bottle. I guess I could have given it a name over the years. I am that girl that names objects. Blame it on my messed-up childhood; I had to make friends somewhere. Ha.

I can't imagine not having that rubber bottle suffering from back pain, shoulder pain, neck pain, and heart pain. I can't imagine life without it. I am not even being dramatic when I say that out loud. I even travel with it. I might be a little attached.

You know what, tea and my water bottle have been a great reminder to stay present and to enjoy the moments. It is those kinds of ordinary habits created over the years that matter. Also, that tea kettle does scream at you. That will snap you out of your daze. Everyone is racing to the kitchen to turn it off because no one wants to hear a high-pitched scream, I mean whistling tea kettle for too long. These are the moments that I am talking about. You can't always plan it; you just live and let the moments happen.

We moved into my current house sixteen years ago, as I type this chapter. My sweet baby girl was brewing in my belly. I know she was taking swimming lessons from God. That little girl could have been a water birth if I wasn't such a scaredy-cat, besides the fact it was most likely illegal in Alabama. All she knows is water. Her childhood home had a big pool in the backyard. All she had to do was look out of her window and see the sparkling water.

Who needs curtains down in the living room when they are facing my backyard? I would rather have a twenty-four-seven water view! My family sacrificed a bit for the pool, and it took up most of our backyard. We picked out the bluest pool liner we could find because it gave us the illusion of the crystal blue ocean. The best part, no fear of sea creatures, especially those big finned with big teeth, better known as sharks. We have seen many frogs and only a few snakes.

The part that makes me sad is the dead frogs. I know they get stuck and can't get out. I am sure when they jumped in the water they didn't think they would never get out. It makes my whole family happy when we find those frogs with a lot of life-fighting for their way out of the pool. I have seen my teens save a frog or two. This happiness comes because they got to scoop them up and help rescue them.

You know who also rescues us, Jesus. These thoughts were stirring around. If you ever feel like one of those frogs, fighting for your life, just keep fighting because Jesus is waiting to rescue you. He has been an anchor to hold me in place during turbulent and trying times when I could have let the storms of life blow me away or bury me alive.

Normally I set aside time at night to write when the house is quiet. This particular day, I felt this message stirring, kind of like that pine straw that falls in my pool. When the jets are on, the pine straw finds its way piled up in the baskets for us to dump the next morning. This is what my writing feels like. I have to dump the new thoughts and inspiration as I get them so they don't crowd my mind. I am making room for new to emerge.

Most people don't realize how good water is for them. It is an essential part of our living. Water is full of important nutrients. You need it to stay alive! For most of us, water is readily accessible. You can turn on your facet and drip. Most refrigerators come with water, you push a button, and water comes out. You can go out to your backyard and turn on the good ole hose and drink water like you did when you were a kid. I know what is wrong with us now; we aren't drinking water from a hose. Ha.

Endless options for drinking water. So many bottled water now you can purchase. Did I mention that water is readily accessible? I know some countries still struggle with getting fresh water. I am sorry for those places and people. I do know many ministries have dug wells to reach clean, safe water to nourish their people. So, tell me, why do we as a whole have a problem drinking water? Why is water one of the least utilized resources?

You want to solve your hydration issues, drink water! You want more energy, put a slice of lemon in your glass or not; just drink the water! You want to help with your constipation challenges, drink yo water already.

The only thing that tastes better that fresh water is the living pure water! The living water that Jesus provides. The woman at the well in the book of John is a great example of one who lived thirsty her whole life until an encounter with Jesus. She knew there had to be more, but she didn't know how to find the "more."

You might be in that place right now; you know there is more in your life. You have been crying out to God. If He doesn't change your circumstances, then what is the point of living? Maybe, you are at a crossroads and praying about this next big move. It might be a new job, a new relationship, or a new location to live. That young girl didn't know how much her life was going to change that day she encountered Jesus. We don't know what her prayer was leading up to it. I might not know your heart cry, but God does. He captures every tear and hears every prayer.

Another story is my sweet Josie Hope thought that someone would want to take a bath after her. I know that is gross. She left her water, and I knocked on her door with the question, "Umm, who do you think wants to splish splash in that nasty water?" No one wants to get in dirty water. I would not think intentionally. But our life choices can feel like we are taking a bath in dirty water. The Lord has provided fresh, clean water for us. This water is available daily to you and to me. He doesn't expect us to save the water from the day before to use.

I do get there are other countries that can't always get fresh water. I am talking to my spoiled American women who have first-class issues like, "Oh, where is my Evian water or my spar-kling water?" Don't forget the fresh lemon wedges on the side; that would be me! I am not going to point any fingers without first turning my finger around to myself. I am the girl at restaurants who says, "Can I get a glass of water, please? With no ice and lemon." Yep, because I am learning cold water is harder for our bodies to digest. Another friendly reminder, the water Jesus provides for us can be hot, cold, and warm cause no matter what, the temperature is just right! Can I get an amen?

Y'all, I have a serious problem here. There are many times I am reading or sleeping; I do take naps in the tub with the soothing sound of the jets singing to me. Yes, so during these times, my bathwater gets cold. I do add more hot water. Of course, you have to wait a bit for the water heater to get hot again, but I get lost in my book, who is counting the time. My hubs would say it all sounds like my personal problems. I say leave me alone in my splish splash time.

"To the thirsty I will give water without cost from the spring of the water of life" (Revelation 21:6, NIV).

GET OUT OF THE SHALLOW

"Mom, get out of the shallow!" These were the words screamed at me by my wild child, who happened to only be fifteen years old. The stuff that comes out of her mouth is beyond my

understanding some days! This particular day, I started feeling a stirring in my spirit when these

words sat on my heart! I do have to share with you she yelled this to me about ten times in ten minutes. I guess Josie was trying to get my attention because she thought I was in danger or maybe her lack of trusting me on the paddle board. I did look a bit out of my comfort, even with a cute swimsuit on. That cute just didn't cut it out in open waters. I think Josie saw me as somewhat of a novice paddleboarder and thought I needed some guidance. I hate to admit, she was right.

About three to four years had passed since the last time I was sitting on a paddleboard.

I mentioned this was the year my sweet mother-in-law's body and mind were being ravished by dementia. I knew if she was going to be able to travel again, then I had to make it happen! Granny seemed to love the water even though she never learned how to swim. So here we were in Florida, spending a week on the bay with Granny bear. She didn't have to step foot in the water and still enjoyed the view.

I knew my teens would be bored if I didn't plan some kind of water activity. We just happened to hear about a guy who was selling his paddleboards. This wasn't just any guy but one of my husband's friends whom he knew very well. He even trusted us enough to let us take the boards without paying him. He wanted us to be able to try them out first and make sure we wanted to buy them. I think deep down, he knew we would be hooked and didn't have a thing to worry about it. We would be chasing him down to give up the cash in full.

The first full day we were at our little bungalow, my girl was learning the ways of the bay. I would say she was getting accustomed to the paddleboards, but that wouldn't be accurate. Josie decided she wanted to try them out in our swimming pool at home. I can tell y'all that isn't something you see every day! My five-foot-ten-inch daughter standing on the board like she was born to be on one. This girl was not wasting any time. After several days of watching my husband and son hanging out on the board, I was planning my own fun. I didn't want to let them have all the fun. My boy even got to see dolphins.

An everyday and ordinary moment is dolphin sightseeing when you spend most of your summer days on the bay and near the ocean.

I was standing as close to the water as I could, chatting with some new friends I just met. I don't ever meet strangers. Actually, there were two families I had the pleasure of getting to know. A sweet family from Georgia, and would you believe, a couple from Alabama! They were both educators who lived in the same city as my family. I could not believe we knew the same

people. How small of a world we live in. Back to my paddleboard story. As I was chatting it up with my new friends, I looked out and saw fins. I will be honest I was not sure if this was a shark or a dolphin. I got my answer when I saw another set of fins. The two dolphins were playing and swimming in the direction of my boy.

I tried to yell at Seth, but he was too far away to really hear me until I turned up the "mom voice." Y'all moms know you can yell your kids' names into the next town. Ha! I screamed Seth's name, and he waved, not realizing what was coming his way. Then I waved back with an added hand movement to signal him to look behind where he was! I am not sure what he thought my interpretation was because he continued to wave like nothing was wrong. I am sure he was thinking, *Can you chill, Mom!* I couldn't chill until I let him know he was in the midst of God's winks.

I saw him turn his board around, and he quickly paddled toward the dolphins. The dolphins were going towards him; this would be a very cool collision. I don't really mean that! (well, maybe.) My boy was holding off a bit. I think he was a bit scared being so close to the beautiful creatures. I was jumping up and down, well, not really, but my spirit was when I saw the front row seat Seth had with these beauties.

I think our relationship with God can feel like Seth's experience with seeing dolphins. He was so close to them and didn't even realize it. The closer he got, the more afraid he became.

Have you ever felt like that with God? You were afraid to get too close. Maybe, you didn't feel deserving. I know I have been there a time or two. Oh, God, there are more important people who need your time and have worse problems than me. These are some of the thoughts I have dealt with. You are not alone if you've had the same thoughts!

I, for real, would have been peeing all down my bathing suit if I was Seth and about to collide with dolphins! Fear mixed with adrenaline would have taken over, and I probably would have a few seconds of that insanity. Count backward to fifteen and just do it kind of action. I wouldn't have been able to sleep knowing I was so close but scared to get closer. It is easier to say with my dolphin watching at safety distance from the shore.

Shall we swap bucket lists? One of mine is swimming with dolphins.

I am not even trying to schedule it where the dolphins are trained and confined to a small area. I am all about the wild ones that are free! I have always been drawn to the wild ones, even when it comes to animals!

This same week in Florida, I encountered my winged friends. The ones who demand your attention. I have this fascination with eagles. So, we will call these my ocean eagles. My husband likes to correct me and tell me they are not eagles. Their proper names are osprey. I still call them my ocean eagles.

This particular time my husband and my daughter were on their paddle boards. I was again left on the shore watching. I was totally okay with this because I spent about three hours in bed with excruciating back pain. We were in Florida; I was ready to be in the sunshine. This would be my family's last full day. I didn't want to spend it in bed. I could barely see the water. I asked my daughter to move the couch pillow in our bungalow because it was blocking the beautiful bay.

I was determined to get up and enjoy time outdoors. I was still in pain, but nothing like the sunshine. My mission when I finally got up was to find the perfect bathing suit for this perfect day in my mind. It was perfect in my mind because of all the fun I envisioned. We all know where this illusion of perfection can take us. It will take us to the same place the current tried to steer me, right dab smack into the rocks. Josie was seeing my paddleboard headed for danger and tried to warn me every time she yelled, "Mom, get out of the shallow!"

How does this relate to your relationship with God? How many times have you heard a

warning to get out of whatever your rocks might represent? Those rocks you keep bumping into. God wants you to move away from them! Are your ears even open to the voice of God?

Or has life hardened your heart and closed off your spiritual ears?

DEEP CALLS TO DEEP

"Words of wisdom are like a fresh, flowing brook—like deep waters that spring forth from within, bubbling up inside the one with understanding" (Proverbs 18:4, TPT).

Are you a person who likes to hang out on the steps in a swimming pool? Or are you the one who jumps right in? You might be the one who goes straight to the diving board. If the last two describe you, then you have found yourself in the deep waters. One isn't going to jump in unless they know the water is deep enough. If you jump in the shallow, then you will be hurting. It isn't going to be a good day for you. Y'all get my point, right!

The "Oceans" song by Hillsong is one of my all-time favorites! I have played that song more than any other song.

It has been my "go-to" in sad times and happy times. I found this song on repeat in those wilderness, valley, and mountaintop days.

I would encourage you to listen to the song, pay attention to the lyrics.

You call me out upon the waters

The great unknown where feet may fail

And there I find You in the mystery

In oceans deep, my faith will stand

…Spirit lead me where my trust is without borders

Let me walk upon the waters

Wherever You would call me

Take me deeper than my feet could ever wander

And my faith with me made stronger

In the presence of my Savior

Hillsong United, "Oceans"

These are the beginning of the lyrics and the chorus. What a song to sing over you on a lonely day. The days of Tim deploying got me the most. Good ole military, we never really knew the exact date when he would come home.

Some nights, I went to bed feeling so much sadness. I knew my husband was on a mission, and he had work to do. The six years I was enlisted, I had the inside scoop, so I thought. I knew in my head that my guy was not leaving me by choice, but my heart wasn't getting the same message. My heart felt pain and abandonment. Every time Tim deployed, God took me on a journey of deeper healing. You ask why because, apparently, I still needed it!

Do you have your own song? If not, then what are you waiting for?

Have you ever heard that expression, you are up a creek without a paddle? It is kind of an old-school expression. With the Lord, we will always have a paddle. The challenge comes in how we use that paddle.

It was my turn to go paddle boarding with my husband. I was so excited it was just him and me, finally some one-on-one time. Right when we get out in the water, he was fussing at me. Or so I thought, he was trying to teach me, but my stubborn self wasn't listening. But he was right. My paddling didn't get me anywhere; I was holding the paddle the wrong way.

You would think it didn't matter, but try being the one holding it and working harder than necessary. I would say this was one example of a hundred-plus in my life where I did things the hard way. I could find the long path. I would tend to complicate matters just a little and cause unnecessary confusion.

I went through a season where my text messages were a mess. I mean, I might have two friends with the same name. I would accidentally text the wrong one. Thankfully my friends were gracious and texted me back. One particular friend said, "Did you mean this for me?" I was thanking another friend for stopping by. Well, the one who responded lived in another state. I am sure she was a bit confused.

The cool thing about God is He will use your mistakes for His good. This opened up a new conversation and cool connection. I really needed the wisdom, support, prayers, and encouragement from her. God knew. God saw my mess up really was a blessing in disguise.

I know many of you have messed way more than a little text mix-up. Oh, believe me, I have to, but the text story reconnected a friendship I didn't even know how much I was missing. We would share many intimate prayers. She was on the other side of the world, still in the states but helped walk beside me in the battle with my mother-in-law. I am still humbled to think how God brought this sweet, Beautiful Warrior back into my life.

Life can be so trying, and it is those times, I feel loved. You need those light-hearted times to make it through the gut-wrenching seasons.

"The purposes of a person's heart are deep waters, but one who has insight draws them out" (Proverbs 20:5, NIV).

Seasons come, and seasons go! This time of my life, when writing this chapter, I was in a season of celebration! The Lord was showing me through dreams at night, conversations during the day, and visions everywhere I went, a season to celebrate!

He revealed to me that He was giving me the deep desires of my heart! He was stirring up and manifesting things only He knew. I didn't even fully know what some of those deep things were until He gave them to me.

Have you thought about the deep desires of your heart? Are there dreams you have not shared with a single soul? Maybe you have that one or two who you confide in. Or you might be scared to share because of betrayal; someone hurt you and broke your trust. I get it! I don't have to tell you my betrayal stories, but I will say again, I get it! I see you!

I feel this is a new season of renewal. God wants to renew desires, dreams, dead spaces within. He wants you to believe in His renewing power.

"But those who hope in the Lord will renew their strength. They will soar on wings like eagles; they will run and not grow weary" (Isaiah 40:31, NIV).

When I read that verse about eagles, I am reminded of what eagles do and what they eat. They don't eat dead things like buzzards. Eagles eat things that are alive, like rodents running around on the ground. They also don't get to escape the storms of life; they fly higher because they use the winds of the storms to elevate them. Has anyone ever told you to keep a heavenly perspective? To look above your circumstances and situation? This eagle verse fits right in; to have an eye view of an eagle.

Have you ever been at a loss for words? You didn't know what to say or what to do? In these moments, I only have energy and clarity for one word, Jesus! When I am feeling down and

confused, I declare these four words.

Jesus, I love You!

Jesus, I love You!

Jesus, I love You!

Jesus, I love You!

Jesus, I love You!

Have you ever just cried out these four words, "Jesus, I love You!"?

The miraculous thing is you might actually start believing it. When you say these words, maybe you have some apprehension and doubt. God ain't worried about that! He can handle whatever thoughts are swirling around in your head. Remember, silly one, He created you!

"The Lord is my best friend and my shepherd. I always have

more than enough" (Psalm 23:1, TPT) (paraphrased by the author).

Have you ever looked at God as a best friend? Like, for real? You don't have to feel bad if you have not! This whole God thing might be new to you, and you are thinking you picked up the wrong book with all of this Lord and Jesus talk. Nah, fam, as my teens would say, "You are in the right place at the right time!"

The Lord has set you up even if you don't believe in Him! Again, He isn't worried about your little belief issues. At least not at this moment. If you keep pressing in with Him, then you will experience for yourself the sweet love He has for you.

My journey has led me to many truths. One of them is God is not human and won't let me down like man. God does not lie like man. God won't ever leave me or forsake me. God does not forget my name. God loves me for me, not for what I can do for Him. Of course, the greatest way you can express your thanks to God is to live out the rest of your days with purpose.

I really do believe the deep need for water is the same with purpose. You have not fully lived the abundant (zoe) life until you discover why you were born! I have heard many people say, next to the day we were born, your birthday is the day you accept Jesus. But that just isn't enough at times. I feel the suicide rate would go down if people knew why they existed! Why do you exist? What did God make you to do on this earth?

I have a dog named Zoe-belle Joy. She was a rescue dog from the pound. My husband picked her out. She was an anniversary gift in the year 2015. Zoe-belle is playful, fun, protective, and a great companion. She knows why she exists, and she is very loved. I secretly wanted more children, but God blessed Tim and me only with two. He knew best not me! I would have had a houseful of children. LOL.

I gave her the middle name Joy because if I had another baby girl, she would have been given the name Joy. I know God was talking to me years ago about the beauty of joy. Back to Zoe-belle's story, she knows why she exists. Imagine if the world was like Zoe-belle. I know it might sound silly because I am talking about a dog. Think about your own life. Are you living the zoe life Jesus died for?

HELPING HANDS

Healing comes in so many forms. You might see healing on earth, and it might be on the other side in heaven. We are not God, and I am reminded of that over and over again. Healing takes teamwork too. It took my man's vision and my action steps. You know life takes two to tango! One mind is always better than one.

I found out my sweet widowed neighbor had cancer in 2020. We knew something was up because she stopped going outside. She was a night owl and liked to sleep during the day. You ask me how I know because I, too, am a night owl, but I don't sleep all day. I take little naps that keep me going. This sweet lady was doing better, or so I thought. It had been months since we saw her.

This particular night I was looking for something to eat. I ate a big lunch and was full for the rest of the day until I wasn't. It was after 8 p.m., and I usually don't eat past 7:30 p.m. on the weekdays. I saw a big bowl of watermelon calling my name! I had to dig in!

First, I had something to take care of. I felt God nudging me. There was a large zip lock bag full of leftover Boston butt. My husband was getting ready to go out of town for two weeks. We were eating BBQ sandwiches that week. I knew my stomach couldn't handle one more bit!

My teens were a bit spoiled and didn't eat a lot of leftovers. I asked Tim what we were going to do with the rest of it. Who could we give it to? He said, "Why don't you take it next door?" This was the nudging I was feeling; God wanted me to do something. I took a conversation with Tim to figure it out.

I didn't know if they had buns, so I filled up four hamburger buns with Boston butt. I put on my shoes and pranced myself over to our neighbor's house. I yelled at my daughter to see if she wanted to go with me. I should have known she would tell me "No." I said, "Well, it's dark, and someone might get me." I was totally joking; she still didn't care.

She was not falling for my tricks. Out the door, I headed with a plate in my hand. Her grandson and his girlfriend lived with her to help take care of her. My plate was full enough for all of them to eat. As her health declined, I was thankful she didn't live alone.

Let me pause my story for a minute and introduce you to a young boy who had his lunch; this mom fixed him that day. He had no idea when he left that morning how God was going to take his little and feed the multitudes. Shall we turn to the book of Luke? You don't have to look too far to find the story of Jesus feeding the five thousand. Verse thirteen, *"You feed them, Jesus said."* They said, *"We couldn't scrape up more than five loaves of bread and a couple of fish—unless, of course, you want us to go to town ourselves and buy food for everybody" (Luke 9:13)* (paraphrased by the author). Isn't that like us to take matters into our own hands! Go down to verse sixteen.

> *He took the five loaves and two fish, lifted his face to heaven in prayer, blessed, broke, and gave the bread and fish to the disciples to hand out to the crowd. After the people had all eaten their fill, twelve baskets of leftovers were gathered up.*
>
> *Luke 9:16* **(paraphrased by the author)**

Not only did Jesus supply the needs of the people, but He provided more than enough! We can count on Jesus every time to feed us! All those days, I was hungry for something more. This was a day I would experience the "more." God gave the people in the Bible the "more"! Back to my BBQ sandwich story.

I was ready and giddy to deliver the food but was not ready for what I saw. She answered the door, and I was alarmed by how fragile, frail, and weak she was. I could have blown on her, and she would have fallen over. She has always been a thin lady, but this took me by surprise. I said, "Hey, I have food for you guys."

Her face lit up, and she said, "We will eat this!"

I could not leave until I knew more about her. She told me she had pneumonia in her lungs plus cancer in her lung. A simple, me not being rushed and asking, "How are you feeling," she said, "Not so great. I am winded when I go to the bathroom." This is the part that took my breath away! She said she was just glad the cancer was not on the same lung as the pneumonia!   W h a t ? She wasn't whining, and she wasn't complaining. She was just nonchalantly telling me what she firmly believed! I could feel the gratitude in her heart. I said, "Well, you know I am a faith girl. I am praying for you." She said, "I know, thank you!" Y'all, it was one of those moments where I wanted to do more, but I chose to respect her.

I knew If I started praying, I might lose it! I knew she wasn't much of a faith woman. I also knew she was tired and weak. If I have extra food, her house is the one I think of, and I am grateful God put her on my husband's heart.

Those moments when I don't think I am doing enough are when my heart fills up with joy. When I wonder what else I can do for her, I have to be reminded that God always blesses the little bit we have in our hands.

Let me tell you—this brave woman is the epitome of a Beautiful Warrior! She embodied the true meaning of being a fighter. She didn't quit. I am sure there were times when she wanted to lay down and give up. I know that God sent me on a mission right next door. Who knows what her thoughts were about life that day when the pain got really bad!

The perfect timing for her to be remembered. I know that God loves her as much as He loves me, and He loves you. What I don't know is, was she crying out to God? Was she asking Him for some kind of a sign? Was she extra tired and tormented with negative thoughts? Was the enemy speaking lies into her ear, saying, "What is the point of living? You are sick! No one cares about you! You are just a waste and a burden to everyone around you!" I have no idea, just like I have no idea what lies you might be believing. Are you the one who needs the reminder God sees you! He loves you! He cares about you! He has not forgotten about you! You are not a burden or worrisome to anyone!

This book was written for you! That is how much God loves you, this much! He thought

you were worth dying for. A splish splash can involve water or just be about how you showed up for someone who needed it.

CHAPTER 10:
Sun-Kissed

Your lives will begin to glow in the darkness, your shadowed lives will be bathed in sunlight.

Isaiah 58:10 (MSG)

If one is sun-kissed, you will know it by their outward appearance! There seems to be a glow about them. Have you ever seen someone who was a shade bit darker, and you knew they spent some time outdoors? It might have been a trip to the beach, a visit to the local pool, a picnic in the park, or a few hours of reading your favorite book outside.

A few minutes or hours spent with Jesus can give you an extra glow! I hope my outward appearance looks a bit different. I hope my walk, my talk, and my attitude are a little bit sweeter and kinder after time with Jesus.

YOU ARE POWERFUL

No matter what happens in your life, you are the most powerful when you stay in control. When you keep your focus on yourself, not others. People are not something to be controlled. They are to be loved. My days of being a controlling wife or mom left me feeling worn out, defeated, and deflated with a slow leak. Like a balloon staying full of air, to stay afloat. Now, how useful is a deflated balloon? They are not useful to anyone; most of the time, they are discarded.

When you are so focused on controlling others' behavior, you lose focus on your own behavior. You also give your power away! No one wants to feel like a powerless woman or man. You really have very little control over anything. Things you can control. Let's start with your hair. You get to decide when you want it cut or colored.

Even with your hair, you didn't get to decide if it was going to be curly or straight. You work daily with what God gave you. You can thank your parents' genetics for the hair type, and you can sing hallelujah for the invention of curling irons and blow dryers! Who wants to confess to having a few hair products stuffed in a cabinet because you got sold on the, do you want these beach waves, buy this product? You can change your hairstyle with the right tools, just like you can change your attitudes with the right tools.

Corrie Ten Boom is a lady to admire who chose joy. Under horrible conditions, she had an attitude of gratitude and forgiving heart. Even for the ones who hurt her and killed her sister in a Nazi concentration camp. Do you think she knew a thing or two about being sun-kissed in the presence of Jesus? She was known for quoting many encouraging statements. This one stood out to me. "Joy runs deeper than despair."

Let that one sink in. Selah...

You are in control of how much time you spend with Jesus. It's where you find peace and comfort. It is where you are refreshed and renewed.

I heard a great sermon that stuck with me, Jesus is communion and our time in the world is when we are in union with Him. This means our steps will take us closer to Him.

I used to call my time with God quiet time. Until I heard a great preaching, he said there isn't anything quiet about your time with our creator. We are warring and praying and beating down the gates of hell. It really flipped my mindset and helped me to see my time with God in a

different light. My quiet not so quiet time changed a bit after that preaching.

The time I spend in intercession is anything but quiet. I usually get super passionate, and that turns into cranking up the volume in my voice. I am sharing this so you can think about your own time with God.

What do you call it? How would you describe it? These questions might help you identify more about your times of being sun-kissed. Those times of feeling kissed on the forehead or cheek by a loving heavenly Father. I used to love it when my daughter was young; she and I would share Eskimo kisses. I would take my nose and rub her nose. It was a way for us to share connection and love and stop time for just a few seconds.

I also have memories with my sweet boy. He would kiss me on the cheek and then lean down close so I could kiss his cheek. As I finish this book, he is seventeen and still wants me to kiss his man-cub cheek. It doesn't want me kissing his cheek the older he gets, but he will lean down for a hug. I don't know why he didn't score high in physical touch on the love language quiz because if he is near me, he wants to be touching. It might just be our feet or our shoulders, as his mom, I will take it!

I am not a grandmother yet! But I do have the joy of calling myself a grandaunt! Thank you, my Cali friend, for calling that out! My beautiful niece is very intentional about her daughter knowing who I am. I like to call myself Auntie JoJo. She is still working on those words. I love her so much, and she is pure joy.

When that sweet baby girl sees me, she gets the biggest smile on her face, she has the biggest smile, gums and all. Her sweet innocent love is a gift in my life. I love the days when I get to spend time with her. I make sure I am rested up because we are going to play, and I am going to be chasing her around.

Newsflash! When God sees your face, He lights up too! He gets the biggest smile.

I have heard too many women share that they don't make time for God because they are too busy. I am not one to make others feel bad, but I am one to challenge you to do a little bit better. If you feel this in my writing, then I am doing my job.

You really don't know what you are missing until you create a lifestyle to include daily time with God. You might not be feeling the warmth of his smile because you haven't figured out how to carve out that space to be still and receive God's love. I used to struggle to find the time with little ones. Those days are long gone.

Now I am home alone. The days of just being in my house were for sure weird. I embraced it the best I could. It was also wild because I could do whatever I wanted. Naps, eat what I want, watch what I want, listen to whatever I wanted to as long as I wanted! I mean, I found the wonder too. Some days felt wonderful because I was taking care of myself. It was a season to focus on me; what did that even mean? Most of these chapters were written in the a.m. hours. It is almost 1 a.m. now.

When I strived and tried to get up and get in, the word were torturous. I didn't always have the best attitude, at least not until I was sun-kissed. I am sure God was looking at me thinking, *Young lady, you might want to go to bed a bit earlier, and you might not be so durn cranky.* Ha.

I am sure God wasn't thinking, *Fix your attitude!* He was glad I was trying to meet with him. All God needs is your willingness. He meets me late at night just like He meets those early risers.

The key is positioning yourself to receive. It looks different for everyone. I learned over the years to allow myself to be who God made me to be. In those moments is where you are going to feel His sun-kisses. A freedom to just be you, not anyone else.

Life can feel like a big pendulum. You swing from one extreme to the other. I have been working really hard on not swinging too far to one side but staying in the middle.

A healthy balance is to give and receive. Life knocks us off our feet, too, and the only way up is by a helping hand. I experienced lots of support and love after my dad's death. I cherish those memories when friends and stopped by to sit with me in my pain.

When they didn't ask me what I needed but brought what they thought would brighten my day. Food was always a golden ticket into my heart and home.

Look around; who is hurting? Who could use a pick me up? You can offer a friendly smile, warm meal, or just a familiar voice to talk or listen or just sit with them in their pain.

It was a long day battling the disease that is slowly ravishing my mother-in-law's mind, dementia. I will share more about that in the next chapter. God set me up to be sun-kissed after I canceled an appointment and cleared my schedule. Some days it might be a phone call, don't underestimate the power of a friend's voice.

I think sometimes you are afraid of your own pain. Pain can cause you to act like someone you don't know or recognize. Pain can cause you to hide. If you are a Christian, then you might even feel guilty for feeling sad or mad at someone or something that is out of your control. You tend to think God might be disappointed in you, but this verse takes me back to the truth of what God says.

"My grace is enough; it's all you need. My strength comes into its own in your weakness" (2 Corinthians 12:9, MSG).

Truth bomb! Readers, in your weakness, God is stronger! I ended my phone chat that night with prayer. My friend offered me a gift, prayer. She wanted to pray for me, and I wanted to pray for her. There was no power struggle; we were both going through trials. I didn't try to fix her life, and she didn't try to save me from my crazy emotions. We listened, and we had compassion for one another.

If you get stuck in the mindset, God is mad at you. Let me speak to you; look at me now; God loves you! The one who created you and knows all about your emotions, He made them! The depth of God's love for you heals those painful places.

I used to struggle with morning times. I don't know why; maybe I was dealing with depression but didn't want to call it that. All the jobs and times I had to get up early, I still stayed up late. I just love nighttime. It is quiet, and no one is awake, not in my house. LOL.

Time to deliver newspapers, time to make the donuts, time for Boot Camp, time to feed babies. I don't know what your morning tasks were, but we all had to get up to start our days. Looking outside and seeing the sunrise brings joy! Waking up and seeing your family's face, you didn't wake up alone. My husband is the early riser.

The greatest revelations from God have come when I am going along living those ordinary everyday moments. It is the action of putting one foot forward at a time because of Jesus in you. I am so glad we don't have to lean on our own strength.

Joy is a net of love by which you can catch souls. A joyous heart is the inevitable result of a heart burning with love" ("Mother Teresa).

We all have those sunshiny friends. The ones who are always smiling. You know it isn't because their life is perfect. You just know they believe in something more than their situation and circumstances. They smile because of their faith. They smile because it is their gift to offer the world. They don't let loss and disappointment take their smile away. They don't give their control away to those who hurt them.

I have one friend in particular who I call my sunshiny friend. I can see her beautiful face as I type these words. I know part of her life story, and she has every reason to let life slap that smile right off of her face, but she doesn't. She is pressing onward. She has found that wild joy I am talking about. She might not know it is wild, but I do. I recognize it in her! The joy she carries can't be boxed in or contained. She was also one of the first women I asked to read my manuscript. She is a beautiful gem that has been sun-kissed.

Weeks before the inspiration for this chapter. I love how God works! I was communicating with my sweet sister and knew I wanted to share *Wild Joy* with her. I was scared, but as Joyce Meyer says, I felt the fear and asked her anyway.

I waited on her. I waited for God to prompt her heart to read my words. I really didn't know what it all looked like. When you let go of control, God makes a way! I tried to wait for her response patiently. I wanted to reach out to her and ask if she had a chance to read any of what I sent her, but I didn't. Then one beautiful day, several weeks later, I found my manuscript printed with edits. She was kind and didn't use a red pen. The love and attention showed me was worth the wait. I loved seeing her green marks and words of advice. I felt loved!

I share this to say, God is waiting to give us those sun-kissed joyful moments. Those unplanned times when you trust in His goodness. I was not sure of her role in this project, but that was the next step for me; to ask for help. I needed to reach out. I wanted to be obedient to what God was asking me to do. Too many times, I believe we are stuck because we want God to speak, but we aren't willing to do the last thing God asked of us.

I was just telling a friend that we ask for bravery and courage before we take the risk or leap of faith. God is waiting for us to move then He gives us the bravery and courage after we make the move. God is our provision and gives us exactly what we need when we need it, not when we think we need it! He knows what is best.

You might be at a crossroads right now with your own book. If God is telling you to write the book, then write the book! Someone is waiting to read your story. We all have those friends with hidden talents. My friend would tell you she isn't an editor, but I will have to disagree with her. Just because you didn't go to school for four years and get a specific degree doesn't mean you aren't qualified. God gives you so many talents, and some might be hidden, but be encouraged you are discovering them! An unraveling, a deeper dig is happening.

You might be waiting for something fresh, new, and exciting to show up in your life, like an idea, new relationship, or new job! I would encourage you to look around. What is the last thing God told you to do? Did you do it? What is the last thing God blessed you with? Have you stewarded it well? You might have dismissed what God gave you because it wasn't packaged just like you wanted it to be. You might have overlooked it because you didn't think it really mattered. Oh, I can tell you right now, friend, if God gave it to you and brought it to your attention, then it matters! You matter!

I was reading this passage:

"The Lord your God is with you, the Mighty Warrior who saves" (Zephaniah 3:17, NIV).

Another favorite, right here. You are right in thinking; didn't I just say that in the last chapter. I have so many favorite scriptures. Have you ever gone through the alphabet, writing the characteristics of God? It was a very healing exercise. How do you get to know someone? You study their attributes.

You are a God of adventure.

You are a God of belief.

You are a God of courage

You are a God who delivers.

You are a God of eternal life.

You are a God who forgives.

You are a God full of grace.

You are hope.

You are a God of integrity.

You are joy.

You are a God full of kindness.

You are love.

You are a God of miracles.

You are God who meets needs.

You are a God of omnipresence.

You are full of power.

You are the God who crowns queens.

You are the real deal.

You are the God who saves.

You are full of truth.

You are God of unconditional love.

You are a God of valor.

You are a Mighty Warrior.

You are a God of all the x-tra.

You are God, Yahweh.

You are a zealous God.

Fun exercise time.

I would encourage you to make your own alphabet list. It doesn't have to be hard. You don't have to do all of the letters in one day. Focus on one letter a day. Then whatever attribute you find, study it all week long. See if God shows up and reveals more.

GUT TRUSTING

Learning to trust your gut. What does that mean to you? I am trusting my gut again. I have found this means to trust the Holy Spirit. To trust what God is speaking and to trust I know His voice. A whole lot of trusting going on. It isn't always easy, especially for this warrior woman who had all the distrust issues in the world. I know I am not alone; can I get an amen!

I will be celebrating my nineteenth anniversary! Say what? Yes, almost two decades married to the same man. Talk about stopping some generational junk! My dad was married five times, and more than likely would have married again if it wasn't for that darn heart attack that took him out!

My happy place is the sunshiny state of Florida. I am sure you have visited the white sandy beaches a time or two or three or hundred. My family started vacationing there when I had toddlers—little ones toddling around. My husband deployed a lot when our teens were young. We found this fabulous home away from home to connect as a family. I still call this hidden gem one of my most favorite homes away from home. As it evolved, my family changed from toddlers to teens. My hope is when Tim and I are blessed with grandbabies, we will take them to Florida.

"Oh, how sweet the light of day, And how wonderful to live in the sunshine! Even if you live a long time, don't take a single day for granted. Take delight in each light-filled hour" *(Ecclesiastes 11:7-8, MSG).*

Florida is a big state, and there are many parts to this sunshine state. You can find me playing in the waves on the gulf. Destin, Florida, is my pick. I actually have a cool story about the first time I ever saw the gulf white sand. Nineteen ninety-two, the year I graduated high school, my family visited from Indiana. The state I was born in and still had lots of family living there at this time. My grandfather was dying of cancer and, unfortunately, didn't make it to the summer of 1992. He passed away in April of that year.

My siblings and I did visit him during spring break. It was a hard decision to make since this was my senior spring break. I was not much of a party girl, so I can't recall having big plans. I had a steady boyfriend and a part-time job, so more than likely, I would have been working.

I do look back and smile, knowing I made the right choice in visiting my grandfather. I think whenever family is involved, we can't go wrong when choosing them over fun. Joy is discovered when we figure how to have fun enjoying family.

Y'all know that is easier said than done, especially when family can be the ones who cause us the most pain. Without pain, sadness from loss, and disappointments, one can't truly experience joy. The wild joy I have found is partly because of the days spent in the wilderness. I am grateful during those times; I still experienced the sunshine. It might have only been rays of sunshine, but nonetheless, I could feel God's Son, Jesus shining down on me.

Remember, the sun provides warmth, especially on rainy days.

"My heart leaps for joy, and with my song I praise him" (Psalm 28:7, NIV).

Where does your strength come from? My strength comes from the Lord, our maker, and our creator. Where does your joy come from? My heart leaps for joy!

Moments

I feel a peace

I feel at ease

I feel a calmness

Deep down in my soul

I feel the raging storms stop

I feel the cool of the rain

My mind is focused

For once on the silence

It feels like a long time coming

A time to think, a time to heal

The sound of crickets

In the midnight air

The twinge of guilt

The bubbling of joy

To be happy again

To let my hair down

One moment, one time

To stop the clock

To be at peace

To be at ease

The choice is mine

The moment is here

Joannie Garner

I wrote this in the wee hours, sitting on my couch. My husband and I bought our home sixteen years ago. This is the longest place I have ever lived somewhere. I know this was a gift from God. My home was a place for me to heal and rest from all of the pain in my life. I know without a doubt, I found wild joy in every space of my house. This particular night everyone was safe in a sleepy world, all tucked in their beds. I was on the couch because I wanted to be as close to the window as possible. I wanted to enjoy the cool of the air on my skin. I started to get goosebumps and grabbed a blanket to warm myself. I was embracing this new space in a season of the wilderness.

That night I captured joy not just in my hands, but I felt it deeply in my heart. I was saturated in wild joy. You know why. Because not all was rosy and peachy in my life, but I was really in the moment of *now*. This season felt like the wilderness because my family was in the middle of exploring dementia. We were watching my mother-in-law, Joyce, decline rapidly. Her physical health and mental well-being were not going well. We experienced new things that left us feeling helpless. A few days prior to writing this poem, I had to take massive action considering Joyce. The poem was written from a deep exhale.

Your everyday moments won't always be extraordinary, but I think you have to define what extraordinary means to you. A moment where I felt safe, protected, loved, connected to myself I would define as extraordinary. That night in my living room was one of those extraordinary moments! Did I spend a lot of money? No! Did I go to some extravagant place? No! Was I around others? No! I was alone and by myself! I didn't realize it at the time, but I was enjoying my own company. I was okay with being with me!

I want you to think about any moments in your own life where you bumped into extraordinary, but because it didn't feel or look like how you defined it, then you might have missed it. I hope you can look back now and see life experiences from a bit of a different perspective. To look into new lenses, to see your life from J. G. glasses, that would be my lenses. Ha.

You will see and feel a theme in my stories; if you haven't already, I am continually working on staying present in the moments. When life gets hard, when you feel triggered, and those unhealed places come up and out in your words and actions, then you tend to disconnect from your true self. I still try to love myself in those moments. My past experiences have stirred a strong desire to stay connected to myself. I pray you learn to do the same, and when it feels hard, the connection part. Remember the ways of being sun-kissed.

CHAPTER 11:
Squirrel Moments

Your beauty and love chase after me every day of my life. I'm back home in the house of God for the rest of my life.

Psalm 23:6 (MSG)

Have y'all ever had those times when you completely lost track of what you were saying right dab in the middle of conversations? Ya, me too, all the time! You might be the type who is holding your keys and wondering where you put them or has your sunglasses on your head and can't find them. Let me just say you are in good company with me. LOL.

I also get distracted by shiny, blingy, and colorful things. I really mean no disrespect to the other person I am talking to; I just have squirrelly moments. I have wondered many times, why can I not focus? What is going on in my mind? Do I have so much swirling around in my brain, I can't focus on what is going on at the moment? I discovered a lot of this had to do with brain overload. Too much information and not enough action, not moving forward with that information. I think that is called overprocessing.

Daily journaling does help out in those moments because I am able to do a brain dump to get some of the information on paper. I do think multitasking is overpraised. I have found doing too much at once isn't the best way to live, at least not anymore. I used to read four to five books at a time. They were all on different topics. A ravenous appetite for learning more and more. A hunger eating up new information bite by bite, page by page.

At times I feel like my mind is on a hamster wheel going round and round. I laugh whenever I encounter others who have the same issues with staying on track. I really giggle when someone starts a whole different subject and loses their train of thought. I know this isn't really funny, but I feel at home, in good company.

I literally have a real squirrel story to share. My Josie Hope took advantage of an awesome opportunity. She saw on social media one of her friends had a baby squirrel. He found it after storms knocked it from a tree. The poor little guy was separated from its mom. Thankfully, her friend had the heart to try to nurse it. Josie had the great idea to help out. Her friend was starting school a week before her and would need his rest. This little guy required feeding every four hours. It had to bottle feed. The little one didn't even have his eyes open. They are not sure but were thinking it was only a few weeks old. My Josie even wore her sweatshirts with a big front pocket to keep him warm.

My momma's heart was full watching my fifteen-year-old wanting to mother a baby squirrel. She said, "Mom, this is Tony, and I want to keep him until I start school." She only had six days to care for sweet Tony. Her sweatshirts provided warmth and comfort.

I am sad to share we did not get very much time with Tony before he died. Josie had tears in her eyes one Saturday afternoon and said, "Mom, I think Tony is dead!" We were all shocked but learned from others' experiences; baby squirrels were hard to keep alive. We knew it would be a miracle if we could keep Tony nurtured and warm.

We found out the hardest thing about caring for Tony was keeping him warm. My family does not own a microwave, so we are talking old school, heating up water on the stove. I have a cute orange tea kettle I loved to use. I mentioned it to you in another chapter. The being screeched at part eventually grows on you. LOL. I feel a bit *Little House on the Prairie*, haha. I know not by a long shot, but in this cray-cray 2020 world, I was getting that vibe! Or should I say, every time I use my tea kettle, I feel a bit more connected with the olden days even though they didn't have stoves like we do now.

When I am inside for too long, I start getting cranky. I do not think God created us to be stuck in our homes or workplace all day. Some go to work when the sun comes up and don't get home until sundown. I feel confined just thinking about it. I am sure I made it through my military days because of all the activities outside. Outside is where the survival skills happened. The putting up tents, sleeping in tents, eating MREs, and pushing our bodies past exhaustion, marching and preparing for graduation ceremony.

My family will never forget Tony and the time we had with him. I was recovering from muscle spasms, shoulder pain, and a pinched nerve and neck pain that week we cared for him. Since I was at home rest, I got to babysit. I loved knowing I had a little fellow close to me. He was so small. We loved to hold him in the palm of our hands. He might have taken up half of the space. I know he could feel the warmth of our body heat with love in our hearts.

I can't help but think about God's love for us! He is so omnipresent that He can hold us in the palm of His hand. To feel held, to feel cared for, to feel loved, isn't that what we are all striving for? Aren't those things the desire of our heart? To know that we are needed and wanted!

Tony had the purpose of bringing joy and laughter to my family's life. We watched him grow and gain his strength. He went from sleeping, eating, peeing to crawling on the floor, clinging to your fingers. That little guy was molding into who God made him to be. We got to experience the changes in his tail. It was a greyish rat-like color with a bit of white and fuzz to it. He started looking like a squirrel. My husband liked to call him a tree rat which was partially true. Tony was in our family for a short time, and we tried to love him back to life.

Do y'all have any Tony's in your own life? Times when you were blessed to care for someone or something for a short time? I hope you embrace every moment and let yourself experience the joys in it all.

I wanted to share another poem with you that I wrote. The moments of practicing solitude keep me present, my creativity flows a bit more effortlessly.

To Remember

We are only given so many moments in a day.

I feel the pull to not let them slip away.

To put one foot in front of the other.

To not let strife or anger take

I feel the need at times for a deeper trust.

To let the clock hands slowly go by

One minute ticking at a time.

To remember the value of a dime.

The addition that life can bring.

Not to focus on what takes away

But the added value of work plus play.

One can hide in their homes or careers.

To not be seen or really loved

To exist but not really feel

We all numb in different ways

Too much news can make us cray

The world is full of violence and lots of noise.

The Lord brings comfort in special ways.

A walk on the beach

To enjoy the ocean waves

To drink in the salt air

To wash the cares away

REALITY BITES

Have you ever watched the one you love slowly slip away, and there isn't a darn thing you can do about it? Yep, I used to be able to answer no. Until my mother-in-law, Joyce, was on a dangerous slippery slope of forgetting simple tasks and becoming confused. A year has passed since her diagnosis. My husband and I were at a loss. We did the only thing we knew to do, call the medical professionals because we were in search of needed answers. Tim had a friend at work who was sharing the erratic behavior his wife was experiencing. To be honest, this caused a bit more confusion for us; this guy's wife was young.

We started our quest on google. The big web was full of answers, right? I think, sometimes, too much information can overwhelm our brains. I think the biggest thing we wanted to know is what we could do to fix it! It was a day-to-day journey of watching the one you love change and not in a positive way.

We did not know if and when this would go away. My husband and I took her to see her Dr. One of the first things she wanted to know was how long the changes in behavior were happening. It was the beginning of 2020, and as far as we knew, only a few weeks. One of the first signs was Joyce's inability to remember names. She started calling everyone Tim. I was around her the most and grateful she never forgot my name, but she would call me Josie. That wasn't alarming because two J names are easy to get confused.

If you are living with an elderly loved one, I urge you to pay attention to the small things; they really do matter. The stark reality of life does bite! We have to open our eyes and want to see what is really happening. Life can feel like a dark hole you are sitting in alone and fresh dirt is being dumped on you. Don't let the disease of another bury you alive.

We were lost and confused about how to handle her new behavior. My family didn't know if she would ever get off of this slippery slope and a bit fearful about how far she would slide. The questions in my mind were, *how do I help her? What do we do? Do you pretend like nothing is happening and hope it all goes away?*

Don't you do that at times in your own life? You hide and hope that whatever is scaring you won't find you. You might not hide under your beds or covers, but you hide from building real relationships. You hide from not getting your annual check-ups. You hide from the number in your checking book because you got a little excited shopping. You hide because you are afraid to be known, to be really known. You hide! Hiding has so many shapes and sizes; one does not fit all!

I have wasted many hours believing the lie, "If they really knew me, they wouldn't like me." You might be in that boat right now and feel like it is about to capsize. I am here as your shipmate to remind you; you won't go under. It might be too small; you might have outgrown the boat.

Have you outgrown who you used to be? God made you beautiful in His image, and your new reality can be helpful, not harmful.

Get out of that boat!

Joyce was living with my family. We saw her days in, waking up, and the days out, going to bed. The small things I said to pay attention to were right there in front of our faces. Of course, we can't be with someone twenty-four-seven, even with them living under the same roof. We didn't know when she would get out of this boat that felt like it was headed over a waterfall. To murk the rapids up, we were the full-time caretakers for Joyce. I might need to clarify with you. I was the one God positioned to take care of my children's granny.

Y'all, do you think I felt qualified or equipped? Absolutely not! I felt like a scared little girl who wanted her mommy. I am not joking when I say that no matter how old you are, you will always have a want for your mom. To be honest with you, I could feel that little girl in me start to cling to Joyce, not wanting to let her go. The thought of her dying scared me. I battled for her. I fought for her. I spent days speaking life over her, praying over her, and struggled letting her go. Losing my dad the year before, death already felt too familiar.

In my quiet times alone, I asked God, "What am I so afraid of? Why am I having these minny freak-outs?" He showed me some of my wounds and trauma from losing my mom. Joyce would be one more mom I would lose, and I didn't want that loss to happen anytime soon.

It can be hard to face your darkness and fears, but to reach healing, you have to be willing to ask those hard questions. You never know when the fighter, the warrior woman in you, will rise up in the face of uncertainties. Life can feel like a mundane task of going through the emotions, or it can be full of life, love, and good reality bites.

DEMENTIA STEALS

I was only familiar with movies, heard stories, and seen from afar how diseases like dementia and Alzheimer's steal, kill, and destroy. My sweet grandmother, Joan, resides in an assisted living home in Texas. I have made some great memories with her over the years. We shared so many days filled with laughter. I tried to take a road trip every year to see her before COVID hit in 2020. I really do miss my grandmother, and I pray my daughter and I will be able to visit her in 2021. I will have a lot to share with her about the crazy year, and I know she will be ecstatic to hear about my completion of *Wild Joy*.

Thankfully she wasn't affected by these diseases, but she was surrounded by sweet friends who were. Grandma was like a butterfly who checked on her neighbors and brought sunlight into some dark places.

Dementia not only sucks the life out of the one going through it but also all of the family and friends surrounding them. My story might be a bit different from yours. I surely learned about this disease, watching it take over my mother-in-law's mind. We were thankful and grateful for each day she woke up. Some people live with it for years, and others lose their battle quickly.

Every day Joyce walked out of her room; we were blessed. Most mornings, she got herself dressed, and my family helped her fix breakfast. She could still do things for herself. When the mind starts slipping, I have found the confidence in the tasks she once did slowly go away. It is up to the caregiver to let them try and assist them, not necessarily do everything for them. It was important to help Joyce feel empowered as a woman.

You have to find humor in any situation. I honestly didn't know if I wanted to cry or laugh. At times, I found myself doing both. Some days she would listen, and some days she didn't. I learned to pick my battles with her. In situations that involved her safety, I had to get a bit sterner, like the times she was ready to go for a walk and did not care who didn't feel like going. Most days, I welcomed the walk. Some days I had to chase her down the road to make sure she got home safely.

Those days I also discovered more layers of wild joy, watching Joyce remember stories from her past, remembering she knew how to get home. I was right there beside her step by step; we were in sync with the same mission to get home. Isn't home the place we feel safe?

Home is where you let your hair down and feel free to just be. A disease like dementia steals that safety factor as other traumatic experiences. My prayer is, no matter how old you are or what season you are in, you will feel safe. You will find a way to leave an environment that doesn't feel safe or isn't safe.

The reality of my childhood is, I didn't feel safe. I had nightmares, and I was afraid all of the time. Thankfully years of being in God's Word, I started to let go of fear. You know, fear can feel like a familiar friend but let me remind you, fear is a foe, not your friend. Fear steals your

identity, who God made you to be. Fear takes your future, what God called you to do. Fear is a liar. These lyrics are powerful.

Fear, he is a liar

He will take your breath

Stop you in your steps

Fear, he is a liar

He will rob your rest

Steal your happiness

Cast your fear in the fire

'Cause fear, he is a liar

Zach Williams, "Fear Is a Liar"

If you haven't listened to this whole song, look up Zach Williams, a talented artist who sang this into the airways to bring truth to what fear is really about.

I cherished the days Joyce wanted my help, and her mind was okay. She trusted that I wasn't going to hurt her. I will never forget the moments, the days when she looked at me and said, "You are one of a kind." I am not sure if that was a compliment or something else, but it didn't matter; it warmed my heart. I was one of a kind, and so are you! God made you, one of a kind. Can you imagine two Joannie's in this world? No, me either.

I can honestly say I entered the weird spaces of wild joy.

STAY HUMBLE

A funny story about Joyce, I am sure she won't mind, she loved to laugh. This funny lady had on layers of socks matched with her slippers in the middle of summer! Whoa! When she came into the living room, I could see three different colors lined up on her ankle. She was trying to tell me she did not want any of her socks anymore. I tried to ask questions. What was the problem? Was she adamant about me getting rid of them? Maybe I should have hidden them because we had to buy her more. She misunderstood what I was asking of her, and I realized I was making the situation worse.

At first, I was not clear about what she wanted me to do, so I thought I was asking the right questions. Then I was catching on; she just wanted me to listen to her about those darn socks. For whatever reason, she was done with all of the socks in her drawer. I said, "Granny, go get a plastic bag from under the sink. You can put those socks in the bag, and I will take care of them."

Some days, all we know to do is the next thing. Some days we do not even know what that is, but as the minutes pass by, it will present itself. "It" being the answers to your challenges.

I am sure your weird spaces will look different from mine. The funny part is, weird doesn't even mean what most people think it means. If you look up the definition of weird. This is what you will find, unplanned and ordinary times where you learned some of the best lessons of life.

You will find the adjective—of strange or extraordinary character; odd, fantastic, bizarre

I couldn't have picked a more accurate word for this season of my life. The year 2020, a journey of the wild, weird, and wonderful time no one will ever forget!

Walking around for months with masks, you didn't even know if someone was happy or sad. That isn't exactly true. If you looked closely, you could tell by their eyes.

I did not ask for the dementia, neither did Joyce, my mother-in-law. You didn't ask for whatever you are going through; I know you didn't ask for it either. Life has a way of bringing gifts wanted and unwanted. I do know that nothing, I repeat, nothing takes God by surprise.

Dementia tried to ravish my mother-in-law's mind, but it couldn't steal her heart. She is one of the kindest women you would ever meet. I referred to her as my angel and was so grateful God allowed me to be a part of the Garner family.

I will never forget one stormy summer when I was the one to get up and care for Granny. My husband was working until midnight, and my teens were fast asleep. She wanted to make sure everything on her dresser was okay before she went to bed. I did what she asked; I wanted to make sure she felt heard and seen. She said, "What about this?" pointing to a willow tree angel I gave her years ago. This particular angel was holding a long stem rose. I said, "Granny, this angel is good." Then she pointed to the next angel, and it was one I gave her many years ago.

The statue had fall leaves in the place of wings. I glanced over at the beautiful jewelry box with glazed flowers on the glass doors. My mind was wandering as she was talking, to all the times she opened and closed those doors. I was imagining her life and all of the beautiful trinkets she saved over the years. All of her treasures were hidden in the drawers.

Granny was pointing to it, and I snapped back to her questions. I ran my finger along the flowers and told her how pretty they were. Then we moved on to a small cross. I said, "Granny, this is protection for your room." She just smiled big with a flicker of light in her eyes. She said, "What about this?" I wrapped my hand around the light fixture and put my right hand on top of it. I said, "Granny, this is your light, and you don't have to turn this off. It will not hurt you or catch on fire. Look, nothing is happening to my hand." Then we went back to the ceramic cross. I said, "Granny, God is protecting our home, and He is protecting you." I pray that when you lay down at night, you will be able to rest and not be afraid.

If you can relate to my dementia story, you might need to be reminded, your loved one's mind is mimicking a child. I am saddened and comforted all at the same time. My heart truly goes out to all of your caregivers. No one has a clue about the daily sacrifice it takes. I also found myself experiencing minute-by-minute humility.

Two words that rang in my ear in January 2020 were "Stay humble."

What does that even mean? God would show me day by day in the ordinary everyday moments that year. To stay humble meant to not judge, to not condemn, to not strive for perfection, to trust, to laugh, to not take me or others too seriously, to love, to tear down the walls around my heart, to be still, to not have all of the answers, to embrace not resist, to let go, to learn new skills, to stay a student of life.

I know I was not caring for Granny in my own strength. In God's strength, we can do all things. I have referenced that truth many times in this book. It was a lifeline in the 90s and kept me anchored. I love that God's Word is not like a loaf of bread that grows stale and moldy if not used. God's Word brings life, love, and healing. It never ever goes out of style. His words will also be relevant in our lives no matter what the current fashion. To read your Bible, to study the Word, to meditate on truth will always be beneficial and worth the cost!

I am still caring for Joyce and wouldn't call it the happiest of times, but I will share and declare I experienced a wild joy that I didn't know was possible. To surrender daily and forgive because the other person's personality has changed, absolutely you feel parched in hot and dry spaces, the strong winds of the wilderness blowing you to and fro.

It was a season of many lessons and still is. I was taught so many lessons and reminded joy is not without sorrow. To watch this beautiful, strong, and independent woman lose touch with reality brought sadness. After holding it together for Joyce, I went to my room to cry quietly so I didn't cause her more pain. I found time and time again. The joy comes in the morning when you wake up to face another day! You get to do it all over again the next day.

Life provides opportunities for a do-over. Another gift I experienced was that my mother-in-law didn't let dementia steal from her the sweet manners she had when I met her. She is kind and polite, don't ever estimate good manners. They do help when things feel intense in your life. Remember that movie; just smile and wave, boys. For those who have no idea what I am talking about, look up *Madagascar* made by Dream Works.

"Be cheerful no matter what; pray all the time; thank God no matter what happens" (1 Thessalonians 5:16, MSG).

I share all of this because my family was trying to figure it all out day by day. If speaking about what we went through might help you and offer encouragement. So many blessings with Joyce living with our family the seven years before dementia. She knew us, and we knew her. My family was close, and all the years of fighting for connection were worth it for this time.

My family took turns doing the room and dresser checks for Joyce. She didn't understand the times throughout the day; she asked for help in her bedroom. I could see the fears in her eyes. She would have never been so bothered if she was in her right mind.

"Are you busy? I need you to come to look at something." The words of Granny. Unless you have lived this disease with a loved one, you just can't understand it. I tried to find some fun in the situation, and I picked up a small flashlight sitting on her dresser. I said, "Now, Granny, this is for backup if the lights ever go out." I turned it on and brought the flashlight to her ear. I said, "Granny, what do you have in your ear?" She just giggled. If only I could capture those giggles in a jar. Then every time I lifted the lid, I could replay the simple sound of laughter.

Oh, how could I forget she had a big tub of coconut oil too. I said, "Granny, this is to put on your skin and make you feel better." She said, "Yes, you gave me that, and use it anytime you want." I said, "Granny, do you want me to put some on your legs?" I ask her because, some days, she doesn't want me messing with her, and I totally respect that about her. I put some on my hand and rubbed it on both legs. Then I said, "No problem, and it won't make a mess. We can pull your pants leg down."

She said, "Honey, you didn't sign up to be a nurse, did you?" I said, "Granny, I am here to take care of you. I don't mind doing this for you. You let me know whatever you need." She said, "Thank you!" At that moment, I was reminded of what I desperately needed, that this evil dementia cannot take my mother-in-law's heart. She still has an attitude of gratitude, thank you, Jesus, for this sweet, humble, and kind woman.

ANGELS ALL AROUND

The backstory of the angels is I told Joyce, when I met her in 2001, she was my angel. God sent her to me, and I was so grateful for her. I really wanted her to know that. I couldn't help but buy her angels. I look forward to one day being the keeper of the angels. I know they are just clay figurines, but the meaning behind them is what I will always remember.

I was absolutely broken the night Joyce told me I didn't sign up for taking care of her. It seemed every encounter with her changed me. I was more humbled and less frustrated with the horrible disease.

God knew I could handle being her caregiver. He knew when I met Tim that I would be the one to care for Joyce. It is so hard at times to fathom God's ways. They are for sure not our ways. He knows, He sees, He equips, He prepares us for the days to come.

"She is clothed with strength and dignity; she can laugh at the days to come" (Proverbs 31:25, NIV).

If you have been fearing your future, God's Word says that she laughs. When is the last time you just let out a big ole belly laugh? The kind of laugh you have to run to the bathroom because you are afraid you peed. LOL. I know life can be really tough, and I want you to remember that you are tougher!

When you want to tell God how big the mountains are in your

life, how about you rephrase it a bit and tell your mountain how big your God is! That is exactly what I have done with this dementia. You don't get to cause fear and frustration. I know Granny is losing control, but the family who is caring is stronger because of what God asked us to do.

The morning I came back from cardio to see Granny standing beside Tim holding the trash bag was the morning I thought I saw a ghost! Not really, but you get it. Granny hadn't been outside much, let alone helping Tim. The day before, she was full of pain, and this day, she had a burst of energy. This was a glimpse of Joyce, the lady I met who could hold her own. She and her husband were ranch handlers and took care of cattle. She would pick up a forty-pound bag of feed like it was a rag doll. I loved listening to stories of the stronger Joyce.

I know she battled anxiety and was on nerve medicine since my husband could remember. She was a warrior momma raising three boys while her husband worked two jobs, one being night shift as a paramedic. Pops was a strong man, too, who spent most of his life caring for others. It saddens me to think he was sick for a few years before we knew.

Tim's parents didn't want to bother anyone or cause any worry. The sad thing is Granny was caring for Pops alone. I am not sure what this all involved, but I know she must have felt lonely and afraid. Pops was diagnosed with lung cancer, and within a few years, it spread to his brain. There wasn't much anyone could do; he was in full-blown stage IV cancer.

I remember the call we got, December 2011. Tim and I were at a church leadership Christmas party. We were in pajamas and had to rush home to pack bags and grab our babies. We didn't know how long we would be gone but knew we were going to spend as many days as we needed with Granny and Pops. He was on morphine, staying comfortable, and hospice had been called. I remember the nights he felt good, well enough, I should say not good. Tim would wheel him outside to look at the Christmas lights. He was too weak to walk. Granny stayed by his side forty-four years of marriage until he died. She also won the title of "warrior wife."

I will never forget the few hours before he passed. My babies were little and took turns lying beside him in his hospital bed. This was my first time being so close to someone so sick. If my babies were with Pops, then I was going to be too! His speech got very slow, and his breathing was very labored. All I knew to do was pray. I will admit, I was a bit scared. My littles were as close to their Pops as they could be. I felt it in my spirit to start singing "Jesus Loves the Little Children." If y'all know me, I am a bit tone-deaf, but I don't let it stop me. I love to sing and sing loudly.

I know it sounds good to Jesus and probably Jesus alone. Ha, I am not even kidding you; when I was singing that song, Pops crossed over, no joke! He was being ushered into the arms of Jesus as I sang. The Lord knew it was my heart that mattered. I still get emotional thinking about that night. He took his last breath right there with us in the room with him.

I am now in a predicament where I am watching Granny slowly slip away. This darn dementia is stealing her identity, her dignity, and her personality away from us! We honestly do not know day to day what we are facing. A lot of change, a lot of pain, a lot of hurts, a lot of love, a lot of anger, a lot of patience.

Most days are simply filled with a lot!

The joy is found when she has a burst of energy and can join us for meals at the table. The joy is found when you ask her a question, and she knows what you are saying. The joy is found when she remembers your name. The joy is found in her laughter. The wild joy is found when she wakes up and chooses to face another day. She is a fighter, and it took her getting very sick for me to see just how strong this beautiful woman was.

Would I exchange the years of putting everything down to care for her? Absolutely not! My book was finished in the days of Joyce wandering into the dining room where I was sitting. She wanted to see where I was. I think it comforted her to know I wasn't too far away. Your squirrel moments are more than likely way different than mine, but our goal is the same; we are just trying to get through the day. Some days, we want the joy moments to linger on, and other days, we are trying to go to bed early to wake up to new and wild opportunities.

CHAPTER 12:
Glimpses of Love

So I never lose sight of your love, But keep in step with you, never missing a beat.

Psalm 26:3 (MSG)

Joyful days remembering the birth of my son. His delivery into this world was scary! The day he was born was glorious! Fast forward seventeen years later to the day he turned seventeen. Another day to go down in the history books! I am not even sure why it was different than the other birthdays. It almost felt like a countdown to no more birthday parties. The days of buying his themed napkins and cups were coming to a crashing halt.

I think my husband and I knew that our time with Seth at home was slowly slipping away. We had a tradition of celebrating on the exact birthday with dinner. This time we picked an early lunch between my teens' school classes. We also were blessed with his Granny going to lunch with us. Olive Garden was the pick this year! We pigged out on bowls of their famous salad. We might have overindulged in their famous soups.

Shhh, don't tell anyone, but I found a copycat on Pinterest of the Zuppa Toscana. Who doesn't love potatoes, sausage, and kale? Oh my! I told you in earlier chapters I am a foodie. I have a T-shirt that says, "I work out but also like tacos." I know that has nothing to do with soup but is funny and proves my love for food.

I could not help but catch a glance at the handsome young

man sitting at the table next to

us. I noticed a twinkle in his eye; I could see a secret he was holding. I tried not to stare, but it was really hard to look away. I was drawn to the love and warmth coming from that table. My son even busted me and said, "Mom, why are you staring?" I said, "I don't know, but I sense something special and magical about them. I bet they are married."

The way he looked at her. He was sitting in a wheelchair and had a home health nurse beside him. I wasn't even sure if he could speak. I also saw familiarity in the way he looked so far away. Like he was trying to be present, but he was being drawn away. This look reminded me of what I saw in my mother-in-law. The past year was hard dealing with dementia. I think this older gentleman was also fighting to stay who he once was because Alzheimer's was trying to take his life. I didn't know for sure, and I have to admit, I was totally thinking about one of my favorite movies, *The Notebook*.

What I do know is there was no denying what my heart felt. I was sitting at the table with my family, not able to stop the flow of tears. I could not even help it and didn't want to try to stop it. I knew God was allowing me to experience ordinary joy moments with this couple. I got a peek into their lives. We later found out I was right! The couple was married sixty-two years. Wow! I can honestly say I have never met anyone married that long.

I didn't get to officially meet them, but I did make it a point to stop by their table before we left. I had to send my blessings to this beautiful couple. I knew I was the blessed one to be in their presence. To witness such unconditional love. My daughter commented on how darn cute the woman was because she was dressed nice, hair styled, makeup on jousting Southern class.

I was telling my friend about this sweet encounter, and she said, "Soak it all up because that will be you and your husband one day." What a thought! What a compliment that she saw longevity and deep love in my relationship with my husband. I told the sweet couple I only had nineteen years of marriage, and she said, "Honey, if you have made it that far then you will make it all the way. Most people don't even last that long!"

Y'all, these are the moments that we discover bliss. It is those unexpected God winks from above when you feel alive, like you are a part of life bigger than your small circle of safety we try to create.

I hope you are thinking about your own life. If you are single and haven't found Mr. Right for you, then don't give up! If that is a desire of yours, then friend, keep believing! If you are on number two or three marriage, no shame, it took me two times. You know what they say; practice makes perfect. You learn a lot of what-not-to-dos.

If you are married, then you too! That sweet couple can be you!

The most important thing to remember is that God will love you for a lifetime! Have you thought about the day you said "I do" to King Jesus? I mean, let's go back to when you gave your heart away to your one true love. If you have never made that decision, then maybe this is your prompting, to just go for it; it is your time to surrender your life to the one who created you. The Lord is calling you! You are being romanced into the greatest love affair you could ever imagine.

The affair isn't like what you see on TV. It is pure, holy, and unadulterated.

You can't have joy without love. You can have love with joy.

To really love yourself is wild joy. It means you accept and embrace all parts of yourself.

LOVE YOURSELF

He loves me, He loves me not, He loves me. Our childhood wishes and wants! I know you remember this from childhood, those moments of picking off flower petals and chanting this. I want you to think about other words. What if, instead of a weak chant, you proclaimed in a loud voice. A powerful roar declaring, I love me. I love me. I love me. Not wanting or waiting for another to love you but for you to simply love yourself.

Can you say it a little louder? I love me!

It is okay if you don't really believe this right now. How are you ever going to start on the path of self-love if you don't start? To start is to do something and start somewhere. How will you get to a new destination if you never leave the old one? Maybe, your start might be: I am going to try to love me. Maybe, I want to love myself. Maybe, I don't know how to love myself. That would be an honest statement for some. I was once that little girl and that adult who didn't know how to love me.

As an adult woman, I have learned to love myself. One of the ways I do that is by getting used to my own company. I told you being outside is my happy place. I love nature! Any day, anytime, is good to enjoy the outdoors.

A First

That was a first

Sitting in the evening air

Wrapped in a blanket

With the singing of birds in my ear

The sun wasn't shining

The clouds were taking over

Covering one ray of light at a time

Maybe I enjoyed a nap

On that Tuesday evening

My body said it's a wrap

I felt the weight of last week

Laying in my chair

This poem happened on a Tuesday evening in April 2021. I found myself alone. My teens were working, and my husband was out of town for his job! Joyce was getting the medicine she needed, so I had no one to care for. One of the last things my husband said to me before he left on his work trip was, "Babe, I want you to take care of yourself." I can tell y'all I have a darn good man! He knew what the past months did to my physical and mental health.

I was spent! All used up! Stick a fork in me; I was done! Done from what? I don't know. Adulting! Nope because we do that twenty-four-seven! I was done trying to fix situations; I couldn't, and neither can you. I don't know what your life holds right now if you feel all those feels above; if you are done too!

It is okay to be done! I needed to be done trying to control my life and those around me. I joked a little when God told me years ago, "Joannie, you are not the Jr. Holy Spirit, so you can take off that badge any day now." I recently shared that with a friend, and she thought it was so funny. I was not laughing a decade ago when the Lord was teaching me some things.

Now, all that I have learned about boundaries and my powerlessness are things I can't change. I giggled, and I remembered the verse in Proverbs. I will paraphrase it for you, "she laughs at her future …she laughs." I get it! Some days just aren't too funny! You might not be laughing now, but when you get bitten by the joy bug, you might find yourself chuckling over times in your life. Moments in your life that were way out of your control. I have heard this many times, don't quote me. You didn't cause it, and you can't change it. I have also heard you didn't cause it, and you can't control it. You, my friends, are not in control of your lives. I know I was tired from trying to do it all in my own strength.

BLISSFUL MOMENTS

I found myself one ordinary Tuesday, skimming through journals. This particular journal I had been eyeing for a few days had a mermaid on the cover. It said, "Make today mer- mazing." It was a gift my hubs gave me back in the fall of 2019. If my memory serves me correctly, it was a bit of a peace offering. He was being a little ornery, and I might have been acting a bit too sensitive. Really women? Is there such a thing as being too sensitive! I would say no, but I know some would disagree with me.

This super cute mermaid journal is the keeper of my thoughts, activity, and memories leading up to my dad's death. Would you believe I found this verse the day before I got the dreadful phone call? The horrific news no one wants to hear. A death that would make me evaluate everything in my life. I spent a lifetime unraveling the lies. Now, I was faced with a true reality; my dad was gone.

"They will not live in fear or dread of what may come, for their hearts and firm, ever secure in their faith" (Psalm 112:7 TPT).

But God, only God, could prepare my heart and yours for one of the worst days of my life. As I type this, I am reminded that our best day on earth is nothing compared to the perfect days that await us in heaven. This place, this world, isn't the end of the story. We were not created to live comfortable lives on planet Earth.

What would your life look like if you truly believed you were made for a new heaven and new earth? I don't even know. I know you wouldn't spend your days worrying about things we can't control. My dad's death was out of my control. I was in charge after the news of how I reacted.

My heart was broken into so many pieces. I had no clue what life was going to look like. I will be honest; life stopped as I knew it. The clocks stopped, and my world was crumbling down. Things would never be the same, plain and simple. I would never be the same again.

As I went back to that passage and reread the words in that verse. I am again blown away by the provision of God. These are the times I feel the most loved by God. I know that I know that I know God was preparing me.

"Their circumstances will never shake them and others will

never forget their example" (Psalm 112:6, TPT).

Let my faith hold you up right now. I don't know what you are going through, my beautiful reader. Life might have chewed you up and spit you out. You are left dizzy trying to get your grounding. I bring up dizziness because that was how my life felt the week of my dad's death. I felt like someone pulled me out of my bed and spun me around and around and around until I had no bearing. I am so grateful I journaled my true feelings.

Looking back now, it was eight months ago; I don't remember the depth of my feelings. I know God was showing me that He was with me. I look back at my childhood and wonder where God was. I have heard many people share they didn't know where God was, and neither did I then. This death, this loss, I could see that God was right there beside me. He was comforting me with His Word; His truth was my food. My spiritual nourishment to feed my weary soul.

One of my favorite passages in the Bible is Matthew 5. You might have heard it referred to as "The Beatitudes." The passage is so beautiful. I would encourage you to check it out. I was in a deep shock with this new reality; my dad was gone. The man who helped bring me into this

world, my person. God was working behind the scenes. I was comforted by a phone call with a

good friend. She then sent me a text of someone posting a verse from this passage on Facebook.

It was one of the hardest days of my life!

GOT STORMS

A day I never imagined. A day that will forever be ingrained in my brain. The pain has lessened over the months. I will encourage you with some words. If you have recently lost a loved one, it does get a bit easier. There are times the waves of grief will come like a tidal wave trying to take you under. But God... If you are anchored in Jesus and His hope that tomorrow will be a better day then, you will get through it.

It is okay not to be okay. If we could understand and live in that weird space, imagine our lives. Imagine this world. I would encourage you to explore that place.

I have told many friends this month that sometimes life just sucks! One of my dear friends said it is okay to say that because suck isn't a cuss word. I wanted to be cautious about putting anything borderline in here that would keep a young girl from reading this. As a momma who raised teenagers, I don't want my girl reading anything with curse words? I feel like the world spews enough at them.

I am not trying to say I am perfect. I do have a potty mouth at times, and that is between me and God. I know some people don't know how to have a conversation without letting an explicit word come out! Some folks don't know better, and some don't care! We are still called to love them. I have learned the hard way it isn't my job to fix anyone or everyone. I am responsible for myself only. If you have children, then, of course, they are your ultimate responsibility, but even your children, God has them!

Have you ever had one of those weeks or days when you feel like life is caving in on you, or maybe trees are falling all around you? There is a verse in Psalms that talks about being planted like a tree. I am not talking about that. I am talking about when you aren't feeling so loved.

I had one of those weeks, the day I came home from a trip to find my backyard looking like a war zone because of the storms that passed through the night before. Oh, nothing much but part of a tree laying on top of our storage shed. This wasn't one of those skinny pine trees either. As I was outside admiring the fading of the colors in the sky, I glanced over at the storage shed. All of the limbs and debris were cleaned up and what was left is a huge eyesore!

A big hole on the right side of the shed. How lovely, right? Wrong! My husband has been deployed overseas too many times than we want to talk about. I know he knows what a real war zone looks like. I was being a bit dramatic, but we had a mess! I was fortunate enough to stay in the states, but y'all get the picture of the mess we had going on.

Thankfully, we have great friends who came to the rescue. One guy brought a chainsaw and his son. They were a fierce team. His sweet boy said, "This is living the dream," with a chainsaw in hand. What eleven-year-old says that? Um, none that I know, except this cool dude. His dad raised him well.

Another thought about your relationship with God. Do you feel like there are times in your life when God is giving you opportunities to say the same thing about your own life? Wow, this is living the dream! I have found that life can tend to feel like one bad dream after another, and those grander moments help me to appreciate living in the dreamy moments. Seasons are full of storms. And seasons are full of grander moments. Stay present and hold on to the anchor of Jesus!

EXTRAORDINARY MOMENTS

Josie went to her first prom in 2021. The way she was asked, the cutest and cheesiest.

"You & me at Prom? Couldn't stitch it together better myself."

I melted. My smile probably matched Josie's.

The following week Josie and I were on a mad mission to find the perfect prom dress. We had less than three weeks! No time wasted, not even the rainy and cold days. The weather didn't even phase her. She had one thing on her mind, and it was a dress. I found my favorite reliable hot pink polka dot rain boots, and we were out the door.

Let's just say that, seven hours later, we did not come home with a prom dress. It was not a wasted day. The quality time Josie and I shared was priceless. My heart needed some one-on-one with my girl. I did go home with a new flowery off-the-shoulder dress that I deemed my birthday dress. Ladies—a sale spells love. It was only fifteen dollars! It is okay; my birthday was three months away. I was dreaming of sunshine and celebrations.

Josie tried on over ten dresses; we now knew what she was looking for and what she didn't like. She knew that pockets were a must. Who could have ever imagined pockets would be such a big deal in 2021. I guess the way the world is, you need safekeeping for your phones because who even leaves home without their iPhone! You won't catch very many teenagers even leaving their bedrooms without their phone in their face. Josie is a tall young lady and her boyfriend at the time was only a few inches taller than her. This meant she would not be wearing heels but flat shoes. She wanted a long flowy dress.

As you can imagine, she was five feet almost ten inches; her body was lean, the dress had to be altered. Again, another area that God took care of! Just like finding the dress in three days. We were so blessed to know a sweet lady who offered to do alterations. This was a bit scary because what if she messed it up? It was another trust step. I had to let someone do it.

The day we picked up Josie's dress, I knew we made the right choice, not just in the dress but in letting our sweet friend take care of the alteration needs. When Josie and I finally got home, she tried on her dress, and I was in awe! I could see all of the pieces coming together. I was feeling so overwhelmed with gratitude as I looked at my baby girl, no longer a baby but a beautiful young lady looking so grown up. I even shed a few joy tears.

I know Josie was feeling the same except for the "watching her baby girl grow up" part. LOL. Her dress fit perfectly! It was the perfect length so she wouldn't trip and fall, but she could wear comfortable shoes that no one would see unless she changed her mind and wanted to show them off. I laced up the back, and she twirled around and around. More wild joy and memories made, these would be some extraordinary moments. I really had no words; I just knew it was joy—an abundance of joy filling my heart.

Life is a joyful journey, and you get to decide if you are going to embrace it. The joyful journey doesn't mean you will always feel happy. Some days you might be sad. Those days you get to decide. I get it; some days are really hard to get out of bed. I still struggle, and you know what helps me? To reach out! To tell the truth! When someone asks how I am doing, I don't answer with "I'm fine" or "good." I tell them. Then I leave the rest up to God. Thankfully I have those friends who call me and say, "Let's pray."

Let's pray! Two very powerful words.

Prayer changes things! Prayer shifts the atmosphere! Prayer heals the broken places. Prayer is where you find God's power!

God's power is found in prayer!

IN THE BATTLE

My whole book is about discovering joy in the wild spaces and wonderful places of life. This means you will one day be full of joy and feel like you are on the mountain top, then the next day, you might feel like you are in the valley. The season of caring for my mother-in-law, Joyce, I was skipping in the valleys and roaring on the mountain tops. I found myself full of tears and laughter all at the same time. I tried to quiet the noise around me and allow God to take the lead. Not easily done with a recovering control freak—me!

This takes me to one of the most well-known passages.

"He makes me lie down in green pastures; he leads me beside quiet waters, he refreshes my soul. He guides me along the right paths" (Psalm 23:2, NIV).

This particular Saturday, I was lying outside in the grass. I didn't have a blanket or chair, just me and my sister's dog Lamb Chop. If we are friends on Facebook, you know him as Sir Lamb boy, the handsome, fluffy, white-haired dog.

I just received a phone call from a dear Beautiful Warrior. She heard my voice and knew something was wrong. I told her I was still lying in bed. She immediately started praying for me. She was calling out lies I was believing. She was speaking truth over areas of my life. I was blown away by how she knew what I was going through. A But God moment...

As she was praying, I felt the pull to be outside and didn't care that I was still in my pajamas. God was drawing me to His warmth and love. He was also drawing me outside to feel the sunshine, the fresh grass on my bare feet! I was feeling alive! I knew I was where I needed to be at that moment. I needed the sunshine and the Sonshine, Jesus! I need to be sun-kissed.

As I lay there, it felt like forever. Only a few minutes had passed. I rubbed Lamb boy's head, and we just stayed in the grass. We lingered, we soaked up the sunshine, we listened to the birds chirping. A time of being sun-kissed!

That whole week I keep hearing the lyrics to a song, "The Fourth Man In The Fire." I looked up the lyrics, and would you believe Johnny Cash sang it. I saw the year 2010 and thought, *I am sure he sang it way before then.* I also knew I heard it on the radio, the Joy FM station.

You can find the song by Hillsong United.

> There's a grace when the heart is under fire
>
> Another way when the walls are closing in
>
> And when I look at the space between
>
> Where I used to be and this reckoning
>
> I know I will never be alone
>
> There was another in the fire
>
> Standing next to me
>
> There was another in the waters
>
> Holding back the seas
>
> And should I ever need reminding

Of how I've been set free

There is a cross that bears the burden

Where another died for me

There is another in the fire

All my debt left for dead beneath the waters

I'm no longer a slave to my sin anymore

And should I fall in the space between

What remains of me and this reckoning

Either way I won't bow

To the things of this world

And I know I will never be alone

…I can see the light in the darkness

As the darkness bows to him

I can hear the roar in the heavens

As the space between wears thin

I can feel the ground shake beneath us

As the prison walls cave in

Nothing stands between us

Nothing stands between us

There is no other name

But the name that is Jesus

He who was and still is

And will be through it all

[This part really gets me!]

…I'll count the joy come every battle

'Cause I know that's where You'll be

Y'all, this book is all about that song! Are you counting the joy when every battle comes? I can see the bigger picture of why God was highlighting this song to me. He needed me to know I was not alone, as I felt like I was in the refiner's fire.

God is showing you glimpses of His love everywhere!

I have said it before, and I will say it again, if you aren't in a battle, then you are just coming out of a battle, or you are about to enter in a battle. Life is full of battles, but be comforted, my joy-seeking readers, there is a fourth man in the fire, and His name is Jesus.

CHAPTER 13:
Adventure Awaits

We find ourselves standing where we always hoped we might stand—out in the wide open spaces of God's grace and glory, standing tall and shouting our praise.

Romans 5:2 (MSG)

Did you know God speaks to you through signs and symbols? He will even use numbers to get your attention. Do you ever look at your watch, smartwatch, or iPhone and see the same numbers? God was showing me 10:10 a lot! He was reminding me of his promises in John 10:10, Jesus came to give life in abundance! Also, 11:11, which led me to Hebrews 11:11. By faith.... no matter what you are believing. God wants to remind you by faith, anything is possible and gives you great stories in the Bible to confirm it.

A manifestation of the current blessings and blessings to come. Did you know the number eight means new beginnings? I was in a church service, and someone spoke this number over me. I was awestruck by the timing and details. He said it was a representation of light, love, and wonder.

I showed up at church that day in full anticipation and expectation to hear from God! I knew many possibilities were waiting on me. All I had to do was show up! God had a cool way to reward my showing up. I know he wants to do the same for you!

I can admit, the showing up part wasn't easy that day. The

struggle was real, aftermath of dementia. I tried so hard not to rewind the words spoken by my dear mother-in-law. I wanted to stay present and not miss what God was doing. It was an emotional week dealing with dementia. My mother-in-law was telling random stories that only she understood. We just sat and listened and tried to find any keywords that would help us to figure out what she was talking about. There were so many other challenging things, but I will not go into all of that right now.

Most days, when dementia was roaring its ugliness, I didn't know how to handle it. I felt like I was OJT, on-the-job training, but there wasn't a clock to check-in, and I wasn't getting paid. The honor of serving Joyce was payment in its own way, but I was over my paygrade.

Days feeling unsure, I had to stay focused on who holds the day, Jesus, my maker, and creator. Jesus is full of love and wonder. He holds all the answers in His hands. He says we are seated at the right hand of the Father.

Many times, you think it will be easy, the "it" or whatever you are faced with on that day. We want answers, and God wants us to seek Him. The answers can become more important, and we lose focus when we don't understand. I have never gone through dementia, but I have experienced my share of brain fog moments. How many times have you lost your keys? You misplaced something important and spent hours looking for it. How many times have you forgotten someone's name?

Even when you feel forgetful, God wants and desires to take us on adventures. He wants to stir up that childlikeness in you. It is almost like playing games as a kid. Think about your favorite childhood games. One of mine was hide and seek. I could come up with great places, and it reminds me of how I try to hide from God. Most of us are good at hiding. But are you good at seeking? God's Word talks about seeking. When you seek God, you will find Him. Another favorite. *"I love those who love me, and those who seek me find me" (Proverbs 8:17, NIV).*

The Lord doesn't openly show us His mysteries. As I experienced at that church service, I had to show up. The atmosphere was full of gifts. I couldn't have stayed at home and found out what God had for me. I wasn't hiding out in my bed. I was out seeking God and expecting Him to bless me. Again, hear me, not about going to church—more about your attitude towards God. Let me tell you; when He looks at you, He is smiling.

Where do you find yourself? Thankfully, as I write this, I was in a good place. You can experience that as well. You don't have to let life overtake you. Your feelings and emotions or circumstances are not bigger than God!

GOT BLESSINGS

The blessings of the Lord might be chasing you down. You can't outrun the goodness of the Lord. A friend shared that with me. She described Ephesians 3:20 so beautifully. I

encourage you to read many translations. What would God speak to you about it?

I can tell you that God chases me down with blessings in my relationships. The day I got to take my daughter parasailing was an Ephesians 3:20 moment! I went three other times, but years ago. I was a bit scared after Josie made the reservations and told me we couldn't get a refund. I knew I wanted to go, especially with my sixteen-year-old daughter.

Let me say we had a blast! The whole experience was amazing! Josie wanted to go back the next day. We, as in me, made the mistake of telling our boat staff it was my birthday. I knew we were in for a surprise when he was whispering to our captain, and they both had cheesy grins. Let's just say they gave us an extra dip in the cold blue ocean. Josie and I laughed so hard. I do have to admit I screamed for about five minutes. That would be half of our ride up. I wish I would have asked someone on the boat to snap pics, those up-close expressions! Ha.

We did pay extra for the photos. Back to my screaming, I didn't care that our bodies were still sitting on the edge of the boat. The screams were my *wild joy cry*! I was anticipating an adventure. When Josie and I were floating effortlessly high above the water, she said, "Mom, don't look back or down." She thought it was a big creature waiting to eat us. LOL. She said, "Mom, that is our shadow, but it scared me." I said, "Baby, I was very apprehensive about moving any part of my body. I was still a bit scared, but I was enjoying the ride in the sky."

I look back, and I am beyond grateful I didn't let fear stop me.

"God can do anything, you know—far more than you could ever imagine or guess or request in your wildest dreams!" (Ephesians 3:20, MSG).

How many of you have experienced a prophetic word? Known to some as a word of

encouragement. I was in my thirties before I learned about the supernatural. I knew something more had to be available, but I had no idea what any of it looked like. My only experience with the supernatural was bad dreams.

I was a young girl awakened too many nights by nightmares. I have heard them called night terrors. I am so glad they are a thing of the past; I still have troubling dreams but nothing like those night terrors. If this, is you ask God to take them away.

BOOT CAMP

July 1999 was a big pivot in my life. I found myself on an airplane looking out at the clouds with a feeling of excitement and fear. I was headed to Texas and didn't know what awaited me. Life had dumped on me in every area, and I had to go. I found a way out, out of the glorious state I lived in. Y'all know Alabama isn't that bad. Who doesn't love the sweet tea, southern hospitality with a styrofoam cup full of boiled peanuts?

I was not born in the south, and you couldn't make me claim it as my home state. The facts about me living there for ten years didn't matter. As I write, it has been thirty-one years. What! So, I am leaving my home sweet home. I was sure of one thing; I wouldn't be eating any fried chicken and mashed taters. I was a bit naive and thought I would have access to a gym where I could work out. Um, if you call the marching yard a gym, then okay, but no, ma'am, my recruiter might have fudged the truth just a wee bit. I can honestly tell ya I was clueless. More than clueless, I was lost! I didn't know what I had signed up for. I just knew what I was doing wasn't working. My good ole dad taught me how to run, and this was another form of running. I had a female cousin who was in the military, and I thought I had nothing to lose.

The idea came from an experience at an air force base. These really cool jets were putting on an air show. I walked by a recruiter who stopped me. This is where the seeds were planted. After a divorce, an affair, and an ex-boyfriend, I needed an escape. Oh, the things we see when we look back on our lives. I am not that young, insecure, scared of her own shadow girl. That girl didn't have a clue of her worth or her value. The only thing I thought mattered was having a man. I needed a man to complete me. Or so I thought I did.

Maybe your story and your past weren't as drastic as mine. I am sure you didn't join the military to get away from your problems. If you serve or served in the military, thank you for your service. I do believe I was drawn to new opportunities. The idea of something being new has always been like a magnet to me. What we seem to forget is that new will eventually wear off, and so does the excitement. Um, when you sign your life over to the USAF, it is for keeps. At least for those next six years. Like anything in life, you do your time. One foot forward. In my case, it would be one combat boot forward day by day until you complete the task. I could not wait for graduation day! This was a day of celebration! My sweet dad drove to Texas to see his baby (oldest) daughter graduate. I will never forget him being there. He might have missed a lot of my childhood, but he was trying to make up for it this year.

I also had a boyfriend fly to visit me. I have to tell the truth, ladies, because what is the point of writing this book if I can't share all the tea with you? My daughter would spit out her water right now if she heard me say that. Ha, one day, she might read this.

A boyfriend, a new man in my life who started out as a friend, came to see me graduate from BMT. Basic military training. I was excited to see him. Let me clarify this was a new boyfriend. Not the man I was married to or the man I dated after my divorce. I told y'all I thought I needed men. We had a good time exploring San Antonio. I was happy to be off base and out of that stressful environment. I could tell something was off with this guy. He was acting a bit strange. Ladies, we know when our men are not themselves. If you are reading this and, in a relationship, where you feel something a bit off, please trust your gut.

Listen to what your heart is telling you. Pay attention to the signs. You think you are in love and tend to ignore those bright red flags waving in your face. Did I say pay attention? Let's just say, when my weekend was over, and he went back home, our relationship was over! I later found out he had another girlfriend. I think someone he dated before me. He lied to his family and told them he was visiting his older daughter. First of all, I didn't even know this guy had any kids. Can you say liar, liar, pants on fire? Oh, it gets better. This lady he was dating. Well, he was going to be another daddy cause he got her pregnant. What was this guy doing? He must have thought I was stupid and wouldn't find out the truth. Just because a girl is out of state doesn't mean she isn't going to hear things.

I did hear things, a lot of things, mostly a bunch of lies that stunk all the way to Texas! Kind of like that meat you accidentally forget about in the bottom of your fridge. You had plans

to cook it but forgot. Or you became distracted and went out to eat. It just happens to be the

week you get all these calls to meet friends for dinner. That meat is still there, and every day that

has passed, it is nasty, foul-smelling.

Yep, the lies this guy carried were like that nasty old meat. Another thing, I was not listening to my gut. I saw little signs looking back and maybe some red flags that I painted a color of toleration. I was a bit swept off my feet, and my head was in the clouds. I thought this guy really cared about me. I won't say we used the L-word. He sure as heck must have liked me a lot to fly to Texas. He wanted his cake and his ice cream. Thank ya, Jesus, for sparing me that relationship disaster. He also had a few other problems. He drank every weekend and liked to gamble. Can you say I picked a winner-winner chicken dinner? Not!

This dude wasn't for me. He was for himself. He said he wanted to take care of me. He wanted me to finish my military training and live with him. He promised me marriage without the ring and special engagement. He even said, "I didn't have to work. I could go to college full-time and work on my nursing degree." It all sounded good, but he was confused and full of lies. He didn't have anything to offer me except false promises. Maybe I was drawn to him because of that familiar feeling. I grew up with a dad who left my family. He not only walked away from our home, but he left a mess for my mom to clean up. I was left behind with lots of promises but only empty words. This guy liked his women too. I was a bit heartbroken but thankful God spared me from that life I thought I wanted. The relationship, the nursing degree, and the lies would not be part of my future!

PUSHING TIME

I didn't know until way later in life, I would say my mid-forties, due to wounding and pain from childhood. You tend to recreate familiar conditions. Your brain wants what is familiar, not always what is best. You try to recreate the same environment from childhood. Again—I share my story with my head held up high for you! If I can help you in your own relationships, then it is worth the struggle of completing *Wild Joy*. Throughout my writing process, I had to dig deep and think of you, my readers. I wouldn't have pushed and pushed so hard if this was for me alone. All of that pushing like birth pains; a baby was born when *Wild Joy* was published. It was not even the completion of my writing because my work needed to be edited and more than likely edited again. Not because my editor wasn't good but because my work needed extra special attention. LOL.

Let my pushing and perseverance encourage you to never give up on your dreams. Whatever God is birthing in you will be worth it! Writing ain't easy, and you gotta cultivate the habit of daily writing. I would stop for a few days or weeks because life happens, and my self-discipline sucks some days. I would sit at the computer and have to push words out. Some nights I might only come up with a hundred words when my goal was 1,000. I had to celebrate, hello...a hundred more words than I had before. If I hadn't spent those late nights pecking away, then you wouldn't be reading my work. My story would still be on my daughter's computer.

I had a nice MacBook computer. This was before MacBooks were cool. I won't even discuss how much I spent on it. I will elaborate on the details of why I no longer have it. My sweet darling daughter accidentally kicked it off of the edge of the couch. In her defense, since she isn't around to tell her side of the story, I will take full responsibility. I was sitting in the chair writing. I needed a break, so I put my computer on the edge of the couch; it was very close to the chair.

We have a small living room. I wasn't even up five minutes, and I heard a boom—more like a crash. I was in the kitchen fixing a glass of water, slicing up fresh lemon because who doesn't love fresh lemon water! I believed I had what it took to write a book. People cared about my life. I had something worthwhile to offer the world. I was feeling so good about it all. Then the crash-boom-boom or boom-boom-crash happened.

I will be honest with you; I felt deflated. How do you get a book completed when you don't have a computer to type on? After a few weeks, I snapped out of my negative spiral. I went back to my good ole handy dandy faithful journals. Journaling was my past game, and it was about to be my current game! I had a game plan. It was time to get back up and start writing again.

I do want you to know that I did invest in a new computer. God always provides a way! A way to press on, to continue with the work you are called to do.

"Being confident of this, that he who began a good work in you will carry it on to completion until the day of Christ Jesus" (Philippians 1:6, NIV).

Do you remember those fun sparklers? I loved watching my kids hold a sparkler and squeal with excitement. I could not just sit back and let them have all the fun. I had to

jump in on the action. We loved to write our names in the air with the sparklers.

Not to ever forget, my daughter was about ten years old and got a little too close to her brother. Next thing you know, he was jumping up and down, screaming like a wild child because his sister made contact with his skin. He took his pants off and ran into the pool. She actually burned a hole in his shirt (true story).

This boy knew where to go to get relief. It all happened within five minutes. One minute we were having fun and then the next not! This reminded me how fast life changes!

My son knew instantly where to go for relief. I am here to remind you that our God, our sweet heavenly Father brings relief. Oh, the times of feeling burned. Not always intentional by others, but it doesn't lessen the sting and pain from the burn. Life can burn at times. A burning up of things, of mindsets, of old stories.

HOW DOES HE REALLY SEE YOU?

January of 2019, God revealed to me how He sees me on an ordinary Sunday morning through a guest speaker at my church. This guy asked me to come to the front of the church so He could prophesy over me. I love the supernatural and prophetic realm, so it wasn't too unusual for me. I will share; it was a bit uncomfortable. If this is new to you, keep listening.

Remember that word weird means supernatural. This man started sharing things about a magic lasso, a shield of faith, and truth! All of this is in the Bible, maybe not the magic lasso but the rest! Are y'all a bit curious now, or do you know *who* he was describing?

Wonder Woman.

I have *Wonder Woman* pictures all over my house. They are where I do my work. Where the creativity flows. My computer sits on the table with lots of journals and books because they are part of my research.

My husband and friends found wonder woman glasses. I just love to be surrounded by female empowerment.
Thankfully, my husband isn't opposed to my strong like maybe even obsession with wonder woman. She is my favorite superhero. Her character stands for justice and fighting for those who are hopeless, helpless, abused, and victims of their circumstances.

"Heroes fight for the right thing. They don't always win, but they're still heroes" (*Wonder Woman*).

God would show me in March 2021 what He wanted me

to do with the *Wonder Woman*

obsession. I knew more was to come, but I didn't know how much God would use it. International Women's Day, March 8th, I asked my husband to rent the *Wonder Woman* movie from 2017 because it is one of my favorites. He went to Redbox and came home

owning it. He said, "They offered a $3.99 special." we were taking a risk because it was a used copy, but who cares under five dollars.

I could now watch it whenever I wanted, and however many times I wanted! This was going to be a great night! Halfway through the movie, I hear my husband snoring. I was then left alone to finish it. God started speaking to me, and this happens a lot, so I had my journal very near.

I heard these words, "Joannie, why are you sitting on your hands?" What? Me! Sitting on my hands. I won't lie to you. I was a bit defensive with God. I was like, "I do this, God, I am taking care of Tims' mom. I am helping the youth. You gave me influence in women's lives with Beautiful Warriors! You are telling me I am sitting on my hands?" God can handle our questions and attitude, don't be afraid to get real with him in these moments.

When I settled down, I knew God was right. I was comfortable, just like my husband lying on the couch. He got comfortable and went to sleep. He doesn't want to see you sleepwalking. I am not saying I was, or you are; I just want to remind you. What is God speaking? Are you listening? He will speak through anything at any time. God doesn't live in a box and wants to woo you with surprises when you least expect them.

This night led to me starting a coaching program. I had all the credentials; I just wasn't using them. As a matter of fact, I was currently taking classes online at Light University to be a mental health coach. That is another God story, what I like to refer to as a God wink.

A sweet friend came to my door to tell me about this amazing opportunity, and because God was speaking to me, I was ready and knew it was a yes! I was getting ready to go back to school and take online college courses. Thank you, Jesus, for intervening! Wonder Woman Warriors Coaching was birthed in that wild season.

Here is the lesson I learned, we have a plan, and the Lord will allow us to walk through our plan, but if you are seeking Him, God intervenes. You will be faced with interventions and get to decide if you will say, "Yes, Lord, use me, send me!"

"Surely you have granted him unending blessings and made him glad with the joy of your presence" (Psalm 21:6, NIV).

The Lord wants to give you the desires of your heart and grant you blessings upon blessings upon blessings.

"You have granted him his heart's desire and have not withheld the request of his lips (Psalm 21:2, NIV).

I would then launch WWW Coaching in April of 2021, even with being the full-time caregiver of my mother-in-law. I had no idea what was to come! But God.

Before that, I would have described myself as happy but couldn't shake the nagging in my heart, wondering, "Is this it!" I worked from home for years and still had my own spending money, but it was deeper than that. I didn't know God was going to call me out and up out of my comfort.

Again, what is He calling you out and up to? He is speaking, are you listening?

I thought I knew what fulfillment was until I launched my coaching program. I knew that I knew that I knew; this is what I was created to do! I found my purpose!

I was created to empower, edify, and encourage others to be all God had created them to be. I was called to awaken women to their purpose. I was called to rise up the warrior women!

My purpose was the help women in all areas of their life—physical, emotional, mental, and spiritual well-being. To be well and to be whole.

DREAMCATCHER

I want to ask you a series of questions. Are you afraid to dream? If so, why? If not, what is your greatest dream? What do you need to do, what steps can you take to move forward in your dreams? If you could do anything, what would it be? What or who is stopping you? If not now, when? What are you afraid of? Who are you afraid of?

Maybe you are like how I used to be; what if I fail? What if I can't manage the success God gives me, which means what if I am good at my dream and I take flight? All of these what-ifs are fear-based. What if you succeed? What if you stop letting fear steal from you and go for it! Go for those God-dreams!

The dreams can only be lived out and fulfilled with God's partnership. One of my biggest challenges was I didn't know how to surrender. I didn't know to fully trust God with my life.

You are not less than in the moments where you ask for help. People are waiting to help you build your dreams just like there are people who are waiting to crush your dreams but with God on your side, how can you fail! God is the dreamcatcher, and He will catch you every time! You only fail when you stop trying. When you give up and give in to those voices screaming, "You can't do it! Who do you think you are? You only have a high school diploma!" Please tell me I am not alone in hearing and feeling all this negativity? At one point, do you stop listening to all the chatter, stinking thinking?

Who do you think created your dreams? God! He is speaking to you in your night dreams too! Sometimes you are so busy and surrounded by so much noise that your ears are not in tuned to hear His voice. In this season, I was not painting much but felt the need to create. I was drowning in grief and badly needed fresh air and sunlight! My dad was gone only a few short months, and I needed to take my mind off of his loss. I looked around my house to see what I could find, what would distract me from this deep grief. I say white canvases that were tightly wrapped up. I was so pleased with my artwork; I painted a dreamcatcher. It hangs in my kitchen.

I knew that my heart and soul needed to create something beautiful. Thankfully, my sweet Josie enjoys painting and joined me in this project. I needed time to create and not think about the loss; I needed quality time with my daughter. Some days, you don't know how much you need these moments until you create the space for them. I am so glad I allowed myself the time to slow down and not feel guilty about doing something for myself.

You know, we can all feel guilty when we don't think we are deserving of having fun. The adventure awaits you always. Are you ready to say, "Yes, Lord, send me, use me! Let's go on the greatest adventure of your life."

Let's go.

CHAPTER 14:
Calling All Champions

I fight for those who cannot fight for themselves.

Wonder Woman

Did you know that Jesus is your greatest cheerleader? He is known as a champion. I can prove it if you grab your Bible and join me in the book of Psalms, then turn to chapter 118. Wait for it. Okay, you are going to miss it if you don't have The Message translation.

"God's my strong champion," verse seven.

Here is the deal, my awesome readers, if God is a champion, then so are you! We are called to be like Christ, right. Christian means a little Christ. Just because the world has skewed the word "Christian," it doesn't mean we don't have the right to bring it back to its original meaning. If you don't believe me, look up the word Christian for yourself.

To be like Christ, to think like Christ, to act like Christ, to look like Christ. Can you imagine what this world would be if we had the attitude of Christ?

One of my favorite leadership gurus, John Maxwell, is known for saying, "Attitude determines altitude." Fun fact, as I was doing research for this book, I discovered the quote came from the one and only motivational speaker/author Zig Ziglar.

"It is your attitude, more than your aptitude, that will determine your altitude."

The day my son got his driving test was the day I met a sweet lady who called me her angel. If you could have taken a sneak peek into my life that morning, you would have seen a tear-filled, joyful woman! I was in the backseat of my truck crying, and I don't mean a few tears. I am talking about who opened up the floodgates! I could not stop the tears if I wanted to. I was waiting for my boy and husband to come out of the building. They went to register, and then we played the waiting game! This was during the covid: it was a cool sight!

Cars were lined up with young people and what appeared to be their parents patiently waiting for their turn. I had my eye on one momma in particular. She had a glow and light about her that made it hard not to watch her. I was also wondering why her daughter didn't look to be my teen's age.

SUPPORTING ONE ANOTHER

This young lady seemed to be a bit older. I was not judging, just observing. When her daughter was taking her driver's test and showing the instructor her driving skills, I saw the momma standing in the big yard with her mouth moving and hands in motion. I said to myself, "This is a praying momma!" When they got back, the young lady had to go inside to pay and finalize things. This left me standing outside in the shade. I was standing under a big tree to block the sun from beating down on my skin. I saw the momma sitting in the car, right next to me.

I looked over at this beautiful lady and said, "Are you relieved now?" She had a big smile on her face and started telling me how they had an appointment for one day but decided to call and change the date to the day we met! But God...

I know it was a divine encounter between her and me. The phone call earlier left me with devastating news; my brother was back in jail. I didn't have a lot of information, but I felt helpless not being able to help him.

My heart was hurting and breaking over his life choices. I

got a text of his mugshot, and I could see so much sadness and a young man who was lost. I was praying that God would reveal to my brother the love of the Father, and God would show him his identity once again.

He was a King's kid. I found myself standing in the same big yard, praying for the enemy to get his hands off of my brother's life. I was feeling guilt and shame for not being there for him. The pain of why can't I help, why can't I show him, how much God cares about him. Then I remembered, "Lord, I am not his mom, but his sister. I will stand in the gap as his praying sister! I am the spiritual one in our family, calling my brother back home. I saw him as a hurting little boy." I told you, I was a blubbering mess!

When my boys came back into the truck, I dried it up. How many times have you women done the same? You wanted to stay strong, and you didn't want the ones you loved to see you crying. I cry all the time, and it isn't unfamiliar for my family to see me with tears dripping down my face. This was my boy's big day! I did not want anything to ruin it, not even my emotional self.

Praise God for a caring friend I was chatting with; she was praying for me and reached out at the right time! I am so grateful for those relationships where you can be a blubbering mess, and you aren't judged. You are valued and ministered to in ways you didn't know you needed. I also didn't realize how much I need that extra support.

Back to this sweet lady, we had a wonderful conversation. She started opening up to me about her life. She felt terrible and torn because she turned down a great state job. She knew it was an awesome opportunity, and she didn't want those who were to hire her to think that she wasn't grateful. This hit a trigger with me. I told her that if she felt it was the right thing to do because of teenagers at home, then be okay with that. The Lord did not want her to be divided in her heart about the decision. To be home and raise a family is one of the hardest ministries. I then shared how I was in the same battle between staying at home and career. She got a big smile on her face. She told me I was sent to her as an angel. I said, "Our husbands are called to provide, and as moms, we are called to protect the hearts of our family."

I've heard way too many stories of moms going back to work when their kids were teenagers. I did not hold back. I told her it made me a bit angry because no way I was going to allow the wolves to eat my children. We were called to mold and guide their choices. We were preparing them to be husbands and wives one day.

There was no amount of success in the world to draw me away from my duties at home! I wasn't wooed by reaching huge career goals, promotions, and great bonuses anymore. I didn't want to miss out on my children growing up. I discovered nothing could compare to the success of my family thriving in health and happiness!

The sweet lady had to leave, so we only got to share a few stories. I gave her a high five—I said I am not scared of no corona. I also said we are praying mommas for what the Lord wants for our family. She was driving off and said, "Thank you, my cheerleader!" Seriously, me, the one who was crying my eyes out just thirty minutes prior, a cheerleader!

I had to get my heart right, friends. I knew I needed to release the pain and let go of my old stories. The stories that said I wasn't there for my brother, more than likely, I probably didn't even love him. The lies I was believing about myself and about my relationship with my brother. Once I allowed myself to feel all of my emotions, then I could move forward. I had to remember the truth too. The truth always sets us free even from being led wrongly by our emotions.

I was able to see past myself and the opportunity to speak a kind word over that lady. At that moment, she needed what I had to offer. Who is around you right now that needs what you have to offer? I was reminded on my drive home that I was loved. I had my son and my husband with me, and I was believing I would see my brother again. You are stronger than what you think, and God gives us strength when we are weak.

One of the greatest champions I know is two women in the Bible. One we know as the mother of John. Yes, the man who ate locusts in the wilderness. Can you imagine being John the Baptist's mom? Less cooking for me if he ate bugs, Ha One is none other than the mother of Jesus. Shall we go on a journey to the book of Luke?

Mary was visiting her cousin Elizabeth. To give you some background on where we are headed.

A messenger came to Mary.

"Don't be afraid! Listen! I bring good news, news of great joy, news that will affect all the people everywhere" (Luke 2:10, The Voice).

Mary was the chosen one to bring Jesus, our savior, into this world. Wouldn't you agree with me, she is a woman warrior?

Then we have Elizabeth, who brought John the Baptist into this world.

You are blessed, Mary, blessed among, and the child you bear is blessed! And blessed I am as well, that the mother of my Lord has come to me! As soon as I heard your voice greet me, my baby leaped for joy within me.

Luke 1:42-44 (The Voice)

MARY, MARY, MARY

Mary is the greatest champion I know. She was without relations; she had never been with a man sexually. The Lord knew she was pure and could be trusted with one of the greatest

responsibilities to carry Jesus to full birth and give labor to him.

Have you ever been around someone who exudes joy? They are happy, and you knew some of the homelife they are going through. You knew that their life was full of pain and sadness.

They were going through a hard season, but they didn't let that keep them from living in a state of joy. Yes, those people!

Listening to worship music brought much healing to my heart. I had to include a few of my favorite songs with you readers to taste what I am talking about in how music is good for the soul! I would encourage you to create a space for music. Music has so many benefits and brings wholeness to your heart.

The day I found myself crying in my bathroom and feeling so lost after an intense therapy was when I needed God's Word to wash over me. My family was walking through a storm no one expected, and my soul needed major healing. I told Alexa to play Kari Jobe. Her music takes me to a place of surrender. I spent many moments lying flat on my face letting God heal my heart. This particular day, I heard what I call some of her old-school songs. I had to journal the lyrics. It was my heart's cry to God.

One song really captured my attention and penetrated deeply into my heart. You might have heard of the song "First Love." If not, please do yourself a favor and pull it up on your phone. Here is a small taste, how could I not share these lyrics when my book is all about God's love and wild joy.

> I'm returning to the secret place
>
> Just an altar and a flame
>
> Love is found here in our sacred space
>
> I hear Your voice, I see Your face
>
> You're still my first love
>
> You're still my only love
>
> …I feel my heart beating out of my chest
>
> I wanna stay forever like this
>
> May the flame of my heart always be lit
>
> You're still my first love

You're still my only one

[These are the lyrics that blow me away.]

Your love is wild

Your love is wild for me

Your love is wild

Your love is wild for me

[She repeats these lyrics over ten times.]

Kari Jobe, "First Love"

To really believe, God's love is wild for you! How could your life change? How would your soul heal and your trauma be made whole? I am not saying you will ever forget the hurt, harm, and pain that was done to you. I am saying you don't have to stay in that place of sickness and sadness.

I am offering you another way, a way out of the dark hole you have dug for yourself to hide, to hide from all the scary and mean people.

Someone I spent my whole life trying to forget about ended up being one of the greatest

champions in my life. She would be my mom. She chose life, she chose to birth me, she chose to

bring me into this world. Without a champion woman like my mom, there would be no me. Hello, this comes with great surprise to me. The one who hurt me the most, God has used to

help me the most. A helping hand to step into my calling. A helper who showed me a life I didn't know existed for me. A woman who gave up and quit the fight. She was weary and thought everyone would be better off without her. Wow! If God can heal my deepest wounds, then I have faith and hope He can, and He will do the same for you!

As I write these words, God is healing my relationship with

my mom. As a matter of fact, I have a picture of my young, baby-faced teenaged mom sitting beside my computer. I look at her face and into her eyes, and I see myself. This is huge growth because I have lived most of my life feeling disconnected from my mom.

The one thing I found myself running away from was a very big piece of the healing I needed. It wasn't just my mom; it was her family, my dad's family. I loved them, and I could put on a big smile, but I didn't want to be anything like them. I was so angry about the death of my mom. I didn't know what to do with that pain. I had my questions, "Where were the so-called people that loved her? Where were her family when she needed them the most? Why didn't anyone stop her? Why did she have to die so young?" I was only twelve years old when she committed suicide. There was a sting to all of those questions.

I knew God was doing a work in my heart that was mending those broken places. I loved my family and the times I was able to spend with them. I loved the new memories we made. I think, deep down, I stayed distant because what if they left me too. My jaded heart couldn't handle any more loss. My heart was tender and fragile, and I was going to do whatever I needed to do to keep it safe.

Can any of you relate to me? It took years to heal, but I want to reassure you the healing is worth it because you are worth it! God thinks you are worth it! Jesus died for you.

My mom was not abusive to me or anyone. She was fun and did the best she could with the abuse she suffered from her own childhood. She also was abused in her relationships after her marriage to my dad. I am grateful my mom didn't take her anger out on her children. I do wish she had healthier coping skills. I know the alcohol, pills, and men were all a way to numb. In the numbing, she lost her way, she lost herself, she lost the sight of any purpose in her life to include being a wonderful Mom to her four children. Honestly, my mom was all I had after her divorce from my dad. She isolated herself. We occasionally visited her family.

It was always nice to see my aunts and cousins.

I shared a story in chapter two about my mom spanking me with a paint thinner. It is funny looking back now, but I honestly don't have many memories with her. I know I lived in survival mode; the good memories were blocked with the not-so-good memories. My mom was a free spirit; she picked up hitchhikers, loved horses, music, and dance.

You have your own. I am so sorry if you didn't grow up with a mom. I don't know if it was because of her addictions, the abuse, or death. *I get it!* No matter the details, we all have our mother wounds. My mom was a fun, loving person and would do anything for anybody. Looking back at her life, I can see that she didn't know any other way to stop the pain than to end her life. She thought her only way to end the pain was to commit suicide. It was a tragedy and left a hole in my heart only God could fill.

YOU ARE A CHAMPION

Have you ever had one of those days when you felt very far away from being a champion or anything close to it? I had one of those days when I was working on some last editing for this book. I liked to call those edits my days of revising and expanding. I could feel the expansion in me and see it all around me. I would best describe my mood as "meh," and I could feel myself about to cry. I was on the verge of tears, and I think I was scared of what others would think when they read my book. Did I really want strangers, friends, the whole world to know more about me?

There was an inner battle on the inside! I had a few mini freak-outs as I put final touches on Wild Joy. I had to focus on what God told me. I know He called me to write. I had to be confident in His voice. I was questioning everything! I was in a season of trusting God once again, in a new area. I guess that is why I had all the signs along the way, to guide my steps, to show me what was next. I was in a season of sorting, something that should have been familiar. I spent the last two years sorting what stayed and what went in my life—a season of sorting through the lies and discovering the truth.

The desire to continue to grow was stronger than my feelings of quitting it all! I am not talking about quitting as in ending my life, no; I mean as in my "why"! Why continue to dive deep into the greater things of life. Why dig deeper into the past that caused my heart to feel broken into a million pieces. Why, why, and why? I just shared with you I found my purpose in coaching! Now life was going to try to knock me down! Not today, Satan, or tomorrow!

I felt like a flower blossoming. I knew His love and watering would help me to grow. The love of Jesus was nourishment for my weary soul. I knew where my strength came from. I knew my roots ran deep. I just wasn't fully aware of those pesky weeds that were trying to destroy the growth and steal the nourishment!

I love flowers, especially daisies. During the year of COVID, it was hard to find them, so I found a new flower I loved. The hibiscus flower reminds me of Hawaii. I have three different ones in my backyard. They are lined up next to my pool. I started to see myself as a flower blossoming from a long year of extreme heat. I was going to be like a sunflower and look up to the skies, keep my gaze on Jesus.

MARITAL BLISS

I can't end this chapter about champions without sharing more about my greatest champion. I have shared stories throughout this book about him, but I want to dedicate this part to Tim, my husband.

At the time of the writing, we made it twenty years together, two decades! I'm amazed when I think of someone putting up with me that long: a young girl who lost her mom left, residue of abandonment. I was afraid to love someone because what if they left me as my mom did. I am still working through the issues and pain.

My husband helped break down my walls and helped love

me back to life. Tim is my one true love. Marriage is one of the hardest relationships to on. Think about two adults fighting for their way. I know, without faith, we would be another statistic. We would have been headed to the divorce highway, the big d, but that is not our story. We fight daily for the things that really matter, like love, respect, and chicken wings! Ha.

Here are a few of my marriage tips:

1. Humor—you want to marry someone who makes you laugh.

2. Honesty—you want to trust what the other says.

3. Humility—you want someone who isn't afraid to say, "I am sorry, will you forgive me?" I think the "will you forgive me" part is very important,

4. Happy—you want someone who is happy about life; it isn't your job to make them happy.

5. Heart for God—you want someone who loves Jesus, not religion. If they receive the power of God's love and forgiveness.

6. Healthy—you want someone who cares about their physical, mental, and emotional well-being.

7. Helpful—you want someone who knows how to be a team player.

WARRIORS WANTED

Blessed be the Lord my Rock, who trains my hands for war, And my fingers for battle.

Psalm 144:1 (NKJV)

I could quote that verse in my sleep if I needed to. How cool is it when you know a verse so well? You have it memorized because of the hours of studying it. The words have power and give life. This verse was a gift, a lifesaver in 2010!

I want to help you understand more about why warriors are such a big thing to me.

An ordinary Sunday morning, enjoying worship. I had my eyes closed and hands raised. Some would say I was getting lost in worship. I heard the words, "Beautiful warriors."

Let me set you free a minute; this wasn't a normal thing for me. I could count on one hand the times I heard God's voice. This was over a decade ago, so it is okay if God has never spoken to you like that. Give it some time; now isn't the time to compare, I was not raised in a faith-filled home or church. The only real experience I had was Baptist. I love all my Baptist friends. No matter what religion you are, nothing better than getting lost in worship. I lost all track of time, where I was, and what I was supposed to be doing.

I was praising God! I was letting God heal places I didn't know needed healing.

It seemed nothing else mattered. I felt like time stopped, and it was just me and Jesus. Then I heard all the angels rejoicing and bells ringing! No, just kidding. I was lost in the presence of the Lord, not going crazy. LOL. The supernatural ways of God were new to me. God was starting to show me visions, and this worship experience was everywhere when I heard, "Beautiful warriors."

I have to be honest and tell you I was a bit freaked out, but I felt so loved that God would speak to me. It was only those two words. I was left to figure out the rest on my own. I can't really tell you that I knew what He was saying. It caused a stirring for more, the "more" of my faith discovered.

The more of God revealing His love to me. The more of experiencing blessings upon blessings. The more of trusting God with my life. The more of hearing God's voice. It was a season of leaning into God. I didn't even know what it all meant, but I knew I wanted more of what I had just experienced.

My military background equipped me enough to know I had to rely on God's plan and seek new strategies. I was talking to God with this newfound friendship. I could say God was my friend. I was learning what it meant to be a friend of God. We were friends for life now. Too late, God, you can't change your mind about me. I am all up in your business now. Ha! I wanted the next steps. I needed to know what I was to do with those words, "Beautiful warriors."

This would begin an adventure of a lifetime. The deep hurts that held me hostage would begin to heal. The lies I believed about myself would be exposed. The Word would come alive in my heart! I was becoming a woman after God's own heart. Purpose began to show up, and I was positioned to hear from God. I am not saying you have to be in church. I am just wondering when was the last time you were truly in a position to receive?

But God…

I saw a pattern beginning to develop in my life. God began to confirm with His Word what I was to do next. I sure didn't know how to do ministry, especially start a women's ministry, but I knew this is what He wanted me to do. I was crazy enough to say, "Yes, sir! Please use me!" I can thank my military training for the courage to step into my warrior boots. I would later find out God was showing me time to enlist in His army.

I had no idea how much my life would radically change at that time. I just knew I heard from God, and He was about to take my pain and turn it into purpose. This was taking place at CLM. Canaan Land Ministries, a home for troubled men. My brother was a student there, and if I wanted to see him, I had to attend church service, which I was good with because the people were amazing.

I made some new life-long friends at that place. I grew as a woman, as a leader, in my prayer life. The founder, brother Mac, became a friend. The whole place felt like a new family. The family I was missing and never knew it until I found them. I think we all have our stories of friends who become family. I like to call them "framily."

In this church, I saw many hurting men who were in a place to recover from their addictions. They were there for healing and recovery. I know God spoke those words because He wanted me to start a movement, a sisterhood. God was telling me to reach out to the women. The moms, the daughters, the wives, the girlfriends, the grandmothers, the sisters, the aunts. All of the women who were affected by the men in their lives suffering from addictions. He was calling me to do this! I really thought God had the wrong person, but He confirmed to me time and time again, I was the one. I was the "Yes, Jesus" girl who said, "Use me, Lord!" You can find this sisterhood, Beautiful Warriors, on Facebook. I would love to have you join.

Some might say, the ones who know me the closest, I really really like *Wonder Woman*! You might have noticed. I started out sharing one of my favorite quotes at the beginning of this chapter. It came from a cool gift from my daughter. The front of the book is lined in gold, *The Wisdom of Wonder Woman*. I almost cried when she gave it to me. The thoughtful child of mine even ordered it on Amazon without me knowing. It is hard to surprise a momma when she handles all the bills and gets the confirmation sent to her emails. Who even cares that I paid for my own gift? Ha.

I would have to admit *Wonder Woman* is one of my favorite superheroes. I know she isn't real, but her spirit is real. The way the creators of *Wonder Woman* portray her passion and fire burning deep down on the inside, I can resonate with! I, too, hold that fire so deep, I fight for the ones I love. I will fight for my family and friends. I grew up being a fighter but not in the way you would think. I was a fearful little girl who fought to survive another day! Most days, I wanted to disappear in the crowds. I was not looking for a fight or trying to get beat up by the meanies in the world. I just was fighting to stay alive mentally.

But the Lord knew I would need a fighter attitude on the inside to endure the pain I have suffered. The Lord knows that about you too. He sees you in your pain. He knows the people He has called you to fight for! He has already prepared the way. Most of the time, God is waiting for us to get on board. Is there something, He has been asking you to do? Just do it!

Who can you be a champion for? Who could use someone like you, a warrior, cheering them on? The Beautiful Warrior sisterhood are champions, and I am so blessed to share life with everyone one them. We all need champions and cheerleaders in life.

CHAPTER 15:
The Wild Changes Us

Your salvation requires you to turn back to me and stop your silly efforts to save yourselves. Your strength will come from settling down in complete dependence on me.

Isaiah 30:15 (MSG)

I should have known I would be jumpy Joannie watching *The Call of the Wild* with my family. To be honest, I am surprised I wasn't a crying mess. If y'all haven't seen it, then do

yourself a favor and rent it. Who doesn't love a $1.89 movie! I know you have to gather your

own snacks, but on the bright side, you aren't paying that small fee for movie popcorn. You can

also buy your own candy at the dollar store.

My daughter was prepared with a bowl of pretzels mixed with her favorite candy. I reached over to grab a handful of her snacks, assuming she wanted to share with the

woman who birthed her, but that look on her face told a different story. All you moms know, we

have our own looks too. I glanced back at her, letting her know I was the alpha mom, not her.

The movie portrayed alpha sled dogs, and we just watched a fight go down over who was the leader of the pack. I was feeling a bit frisky, and she was the closest one who got to experience it.

That young girl, aka my mini-me, needs to watch how she looks at me. Can I get an amen? Do you moms get what I mean? I know my sweet girl got her crazy looks, honestly (from her dad). LOL.

Some would call it the mean mugging. God isn't fazed! He loves us just the same. As a matter of fact, God loves you this much! He sent His only Son on the cross to bear the weight of the world, your sins, to be forgiven. If you want to learn more, check out the book of John,

especially chapter three. I could spend every day, all day reading the book of John. There are so

many life nuggets in it. I hope I have built up enough curiosity that you explore it for yourself. The Bible has been a healing balm for my weary soul. I mean, back in the day, it brought so much truth on top of all the lies I believed. It was like honey to my soul. I could taste the sweetness on my lips as I devoured verse after verse.

I went on a journey getting to know God. This journey didn't start until I was a young adult. When I say young, I mean like in my thirties. I know, no shame in my Bible reading game. I told y'all I wasn't brought up in church. I found Jesus at a young age, but it was many years later in life until I discovered God, the Father. The trinity consists of three parts: the Father, the Son, and the Holy Spirit.

GOT TRUST

When I say the word "Dad," I feel a warm and fuzzy feeling. If you look up the definition of dad, you will find "one's father." Assuming you have a relationship with God, what do you call Him? I have heard many refer to him as daddy, but I just can't do it. Typing those words makes me want to cringe a bit. I guess I still have some healing. Will we ever be fully healed on earth? I loved my dad but spent many years, as I mentioned wondering if he loved me back.

I kind of figured you wouldn't have picked up this book without some kind of faith. You are more than likely triggered with your own father, dad issues. My heart cry and vision for *Wild Joy* is for your readers who believe in God to trust Him again. To allow God to be Lord over your life. To let Jesus be king in your life. I get it; that trust part gets me every time. To trust someone with your life is to lay it all down. It is to surrender and let go. We could talk the rest of the pages about letting go, but we won't! I will spare you the lengthy lecture.

We all have times in our lives when we are willing and ready. I know it took until I had my own children to trust God. I knew that this parenting thing God threw me into was not going to work unless I let go. I knew a lot of what not to do but had a huge learning curve ahead of me for a lot of the what-to-dos. I did not know where to start with having babies. I mentioned the fear, it was a familiar feeling, and it was all I knew then.

Now, this second baby God gave me, Josie Hope, is the one who most of this book is about. She is the one who I call out to Jesus the loudest to! I know you have a Josie in your life too. The one who acts just like you challenges you the most, makes ya wanna *scream!*

Parenting is not for those who give up quickly; it takes knowing that the calling is bigger than your fears of messing up! So many mistakes but also an endless supply of love. I hope some of my learned lessons help you. I have also learned a lot about myself. Don't even think about having children unless you want to discover things about yourself.

The year 2021 was a big year for my family! It was the year *Wild Joy* was finished, the year my family clung to the word "together." It became more than a word to us; we were on a journey of living it out. It would be the glue that held us "together" when the storms of life would blow in. My husband suggested this word, and only God would know how important that word would be.

You can put parenting in the category of enduring storms. For all of you mommas of daughters, you know what I am talking about. I knew I was in trouble when my husband and I named our daughter Josie, which means to add to. She sure does add to our family and everyone she meets. I can't wait to see what God does in her life. The power she will discover as she serves the Lord. Raising Josie reminds me of my younger self, except she is more courageous and fearless. One thing I will always be proud of is the day I said yes to Jesus and surrendered my heart to Him. Also, the day that I found out I would be a mom, not only to a baby girl but also to a baby boy.

"But let me run loose and free, celebrating God's great work. Every bone in my body laughing, singing, 'God, there's no one like you'" (Psalm 35:9-10, MSG).

MY SALVATION

I accepted Jesus at the age of eleven. This was the day I asked Jesus in my heart. Even though I didn't grow up in church, my salvation experience was because friends invited me to church. I am grateful for the friends who had families who took them to church, especially when they invited me. I don't know what it was, but I was hungry then for more. I had no idea what the more consisted of, but I always knew there had to be "more" in life.

Some of my favorite church memories were the small country churches. I loved that intimate feeling of a church family. I am sure it was because I was missing that family unit. Yes, I still had my dad and my siblings, but we weren't very close. It seemed I was the oldest and so distant from my siblings. I am sure it had a lot to do with taking on a mother role instead of being allowed to be their big sister, and, to be honest, I didn't know how to do that.

It would take until my forties before I understood the difference and let go of replacing our mom. I knew deep down I could never be their mom, but it made me so sad to see my siblings miss out on all the mom stuff. I think, deep down, the sadness I felt, I never wanted my brother or sisters to feel. I tried so hard to protect them from all of those feelings that went with losing a mom. I can't even tell you what they all are. I am still on the journey of learning all that was lost; maybe parts of me tried to replace and overcompensate over the years for what was gone. How do you replace a mom?

But God...

I really can't say I blamed God for my mom's death. My faith was new, and I didn't know who God was. I understood enough to know that Jesus died for me, and that was enough to ask Him to come into my heart. I can see now that my heart was protected from a life of anger towards God. I know a lot of people blame God for bad things that happen in their lives. I think a question I will always ask myself is, "Why do bad things happen to good people?"

TOUGH PEOPLE LAST

If you're going through a tough time, I want to remind you of God's faithfulness. John Maxwell, as you know, is one of my leadership gurus. He said, "Tough times don't last, but tough people do." What does this even mean? Tough people last!

As I worked on this book and finalized chapters, that statement helped me. This help was

especially needed during the COVID-19 pandemic. A time of quarantine, a time of Americans

staying at home. Some were dying of the virus, and some were dying from loneliness. I deep loss for the way things that used to be. My teenagers weren't happy; they wanted to go hang out with their friends and continue on with life as they knew it.

I think deep down, we all longed for some type of normalcy. You can call this year wild, weird and wonderful, all wrapped together. Some much change in the year, so much change in me! The people around me changed. I think we; the whole world was due for a long-awaited change.

It was a scary time in the world; schools were closed, sports events cancelled, concerts cancelled, graduations cancelled. The world literally shut down one large social event at a time. Can you believe the New York Stock Exchange, department stores, military bases, and amusement parks were closed? Goodbye shopping as we knew it! The word "essential" became a buzzword. Grocery stores and home stores like Lowe's and Home Depot would become our new hangout.

My husband and I made a list of the home projects we wanted to work on. If you peeped into our home, you would find us tearing down our fireplace brick by brick, tile by tile, and putting up one colored longboard at a time. I was the designer, and he was the constructor. We had fun making a drawing of our fireplace; the evidence was in my backyard. It really helped to work outside breathing in the fresh air. It seemed this virus was sucking the life not only out of people but also our routines and daily work schedules.

Tim and I spent most of our shopping hours online, searching aimlessly. We were not always sure what we were searching for, as most people were feeling the same way. Being at home together forced us to look at one another and try to come up with projects. We also became very aware of little things we wanted to change but didn't stop and take the time to change. Like I said, it was a year of change! When is the best time to do anything? Now. Yep, you have heard me share that quote before, Now is the best time for anything.

GOT PROJECTS

We wanted to create, we knew the old had to go, and I can't say we saw what was coming, so there wasn't much of a budget for all this creating. We didn't have the liberty to visit local stores. The plans we found online sparked creativity but flashed a pricey cost!

Budget or no budget, Tim and I took those creative ideas and used them to meet our one income needs. I have to give most of the credit to my brilliant husband, who came up with a grand idea to buy pine boards. I am grateful to have a handyman husband, we didn't see eye to eye on everything, but we did respect each other's differences. That is something to celebrate! He did listen to me, and I tried to listen to him. We used that saying a lot, "Listen, Linda" You know the video that went viral where the little boy is telling his mom, Linda, why he needed to eat a donut. My family has shared so many laughs over those two words; *Listen, Linda*!

As the different ideas came, someone needed to be reminded of our budget, the one we didn't have because this was a bit spontaneous. Isn't it always a good day to work on home projects! My husband is a DIY guy. He has saved our family so much money.

If any of you have done your own DIY projects, you know that overspending is part of the plan; unexpected expenses always come up. I'm not complaining; we saved money not hiring someone to do the labor.

One of the one hundred thousand things I love about Tim, he isn't afraid to try new things! He will try almost anything once. He is a man who isn't lacking confidence, and ladies, that is hot! A woman like myself who had to grow into her confidence needs that kind of a man. Tim is a man who isn't afraid to make mistakes. I still struggle with having the confidence to try new things.

Tim has been known to quote throughout his life, if you aren't making mistakes, you aren't trying, and don't judge others by their mistakes. He is the type of guy who will figure it out as he goes. Everyone has their limits or non-negotiables in life. My dear darling husband is known to not do anything concerning electricity. I have heard him say many times, "He can't fight something he can't see." Another one of his electrical-related sayings is, "It only takes one time to get bit." I wish you could hear his sweet southern accent. LOL.

You will also never find him working on our vehicles. He said, "That's what mechanics are for. Let the professionals do what they're good at." I might have felt a bit like that with home projects but watching my husband fix, replace, and repair things in our home showed me what was possible. His confidence helped to build my confidence.

I recognized myself stepping into a new season of bravery. This season would include all kinds of surprises. Things I never saw myself doing. I am grateful I did not let fear stop me. What are some things you have been waiting to try? If it concerns your home, I know money stops us, but what can you do. It helps me to move forward when I focus on what I can do, not on what I can't do.

I learned how to stain furniture. I was amazed that stain came in more than one color. I thought that the brownish color was my only option. Tim introduced me to a whole new world in remodeling our home. I have watched him throughout our whole marriage, showing so much confidence. At times I let his confidence intimidate me to not even try. As I mentioned, this was a new season, and I wasn't going to be scared anymore of making mistakes or messing up.

Our desires play a huge part in going after new things. I had a desire to learn new things. I know this came from a place of pain, losing my dad. My dad's death helped me to realize life is too short not to try new things. The great reward was not only a confidence booster but the joy I feel every time I look at our new fireplace.

I see more than colorful wood pieces lined up around a metal insert. I see a willingness to learn, I see growth, and I see teamwork. I see deeper communication with my husband and a few colorful words. LOL. I don't want you to think it was all smooth sailing; I may have lost my cool a few times. I did apologize later. This season changed me. The wild calls us and changes us from the inside out.

Another cool adventure Tim and I went on was to the blueberry farm. We have gone before. I am on their email list. I couldn't believe it was the season to pick blueberries, whoop!

GOT BERRIES

I immediately knew I wanted to go ASAP! This led to a humid Wednesday morning of Tim and I taking a short road trip. As we arrived, we were shocked to see the amount of people already there. We almost turned around thinking about that heat and the crazy COVID issues with an attitude of "forget about it." The reminder of how sweet, fresh, and good the fresh blueberries would taste in our bellies kept us on track to our destination.

I thought I was watching something out of a movie, that strange feeling of twilight, to see families donned in face masks. We were outside enjoying the rows and rows of blueberry

patches. Who doesn't love the freedom of open fields, especially with berries as a reward? There were signs to remind us of the six-foot social distancing, as well as a recommendation to wear a face mask. If we got the choice to wear the silly masks, we didn't wear them.

Hint, you can't eat berries while your face is covered. LOL.

With the farm swarming with people, it was no surprise I was led by my introverted husband to the bushes farthest away from the crowd. He gladly obliged to this new distancing rule which is still funny since neither one of us enjoys keeping the rules. His military career paved a path of rules, and don't ask questions with a heaping pile of hurry up and wait!

Ask me how I know! I would bet that the years of enforced rules upon rules leave a person with a bit of a rebellious attitude when given the opportunity to do what one wants! I think we can all stop and ask ourselves what rules in our life left us feeling a bit controlled and a bit like a bull bucking everything in sight?

I might be known for my own bucking at times, but I am the girl who likes to follow what she is told to do. I do have those small itty-bitty irks that get me from time to time, like people talking so loud on their phones they disrupt the atmosphere.

Picture Tim and I with our plastic buckets taking our time looking for the biggest and most colorful berries to pick. The sun was shining so bright sweat was running down our faces. We didn't even mind since we were making memories and enjoying the time exploring the wide-open spaces.

You know the sun didn't bother us too much because this was deemed an annual event for our family. Our teens decided they were too cool to go with us, but they sure did enjoy eating handfuls when we got home.

Back to my disdain for talking loudly on cell phones. You know, I think it was also about disrupting nature, too. If I could pick, I would live outside in a treehouse overlooking a body of water. Nothing beats the peace and tranquility that comes with being close to nature. I can tell you I was feeling our utopia slowly leaving us by this one lady speaking loudly on her cell phone for fifteen minutes. Come on, the last thing we expected to deal with. No one wanted or needed to hear the details of her conversation. The sounds of birds singing and bugs chirping was what my ears were craving.

I did eventually try to tune her out and enjoy the voices and laughter of the little children that were excited to be helping their parents. One mom continually told her son, "Good job." My husband and I both chuckled when we heard her son say, "You are doing good, Mom." This is the conversation I wanted to be privy to, the edification and love between a mother and son. I know my attitude was a bit judgy towards that lady on the phone, and I might have given her some not-so-nice looks through my sunglasses, but that didn't count, right! She couldn't actually see my eyes. I guess my point in sharing that story is we will have times in our lives when we have to block out the voice of others and not allow outside noise to dictate our reactions.

BELIEF GROWS

I raised a son who was all about edification. If I raised my voice, his bottom lip would start to quiver. He was my "words of affirmation" guy. I loved that the mom picking blueberries with her son was being intentional about building confidence in her son at an early age. She was setting him up to believe in himself. If you feel like no one ever believed in you, let me stop right now and speak this over you.

I believe in you!

My husband and I ended up finding our own bushes to pick from and were not even together anymore. When we found our way back together, I noticed my bucket was not very full. Do you have any guesses why? Ha! Yep, because I was putting more in my mouth than my bucket. Tim was the one who was on a mission trying to fill up his bucket as fast as he could, or not, sometimes we think life is a competition, but it isn't.

Tim led me over to the fuller bushes he discovered. I was hesitant to go at first; I didn't like him telling me where to pick blueberries, a bit of that stubbornness coming out. I did remember my bucket had a lot less than his due to me eating them. I had nothing to lose following him. I trusted at that moment that his intentions were good and for me. I know it sounds silly, but how many people had wrong intentions, and you trusted them then got hurt.

His words "Honey, come over here" has a familiar ring to it. This moved me into action to find him. I wanted to be stubborn and stay where I was, but I was curious why he was calling me. In approaching him, I saw he had hit the motherload in blueberries. These bushes were full of plump berries. With the pattern repeating itself of me eating them, I discovered they were sweeter. I don't know if it was the raging humidity or the larger berries that filled my bucket quickly.

My husband won me over with his generous offer by exchanging buckets so I could get out of the heat sooner. Imagine; the story could have been different if I let the past hurts of others cause me to not trust my husband. I have my moments when I get triggered and have to remind myself that Tim is for me, not against me. We are on the same team, and he is my biggest cheerleader.

As he handed me the keys, he suggested I go find relief in our truck with the air conditioner blasting. I knew that involved lots of A/C blowing. All of the times I let fear control my actions, I missed great opportunities because of past pain.

I'm so thankful this time was different, and I reaped good fruit, literally lots of fresh blueberries.

I reflected on the reason my husband called me close; it was to help me, not hurt me. How many times has God done the same? Is God calling you closer now? Are you feeling fear because of what so and so did to you years ago or yesterday? At one point, do you stop allowing fear and pain to stop stealing from us?

GOT EXPECTATIONS

God, calling you comes in many forms. It may be in an audible form like a soft whisper, loud roar, or your own familiar voice. The voices of God show up in times that we are expecting to hear from God, and those times you are pleasantly surprised. I love it when I see word pictures.

I tend to see part of Bible verses, too, but I don't always know where exactly the scripture is found. I also see visions; these are the times I am not expecting to hear from God because I might be loading the dishwasher, driving, walking for exercise, or just sitting with my thoughts. I have learned the art of being still. You don't have to be writing, reading, or even listening to music, just practicing stillness. This book is full of all the visions I saw.

First thing in the morning is not usually my time to spend with God. I do like to sit in silence then and gather my thoughts. I do some journaling and reading. My point in all of this is, you have to find the time for the things that are important to you. What do you enjoy doing that makes you feel alive? Do it! I already shared I'm a night owl, and those "weeee" morning times is when I did most of the writing.

God's calling could also be in your dream life. Do I have any vivid dreamers? After my dad's death, I dreamed about him a lot! I know most of the dreams were for comfort and a gift. I will be honest, not all the dreams were pleasant; some of them kind of scared me.

Now I can see God was trying to break through the fear in my life. I am so sorry if you are one who has battled nightmares; they are no fun! Did you know that you can take authority over your dreams?

I was not happy to get caught in the act of being careless with my words; when my mom found the poem I wrote in 1985. I do remember the poem my mom found being about butts. Haha, I told you it wasn't for children's eyes. Looking back now, this began my colorful writing career. I shared that funny story with you at the beginning of the book because a year later, I would lose my mom. All of the memories of wouldn't be were gone.

I want you to go back to your childhood and think of a funny memory! I have found these childhood memories mold our lives. I know now, writing those poems saved my life. I will share how. Most of my childhood, I felt alone, and writing was my friend. After my mom's death, I had many questions. I didn't feel I had anyone to talk to. I didn't think anyone cared.

My dad always seemed to be gone or consumed with a new woman. He, sure enough, liked his ladies. I say that with all due respect to my dad. I can kind of smile about that now. He was codependent and didn't think he could leave without a female.

Some of the questions would remain hidden until I had my own children. Being a mom welcomed me to into uncharted wild spaces. Those wild spaces have changed me. The wild spaces can change you too if you allow it!

CHAPTER 16:
Special Agents

We are therefore Christ's ambassadors, as though God were making his appeal through us. We implore you on Christ's behalf: Be reconciled to God.

2 Corinthians 5:20 (NIV)

If we all do our part and use the influence God has given us, then we are being change agents. What kind of change do you want to see in the world? Then go out in the world and be that change. The world needs you to be all that God has called you to be. Why are you waiting for someone else to do or say what the Lord has told you to do?

Have you ever listened to a good preaching message and got fired up? It isn't for you to keep it to yourself. It is for you to do something with it. You don't have to wait until you get all of the details. The Lord wants you to do something now. I told you about my saying; I know my family is getting tired of hearing. When is the best time to do something? Now! Now is the best time! You know why now is the best time because power is in the now. God's power is for right now.

Let's think about times when you waited and sat on a word. Wouldn't you say that the power slowly left? I know I have many experiences when God told me to do something, and I waited. Why do we wait? Is it because we are so busy, there isn't much room left for anything else like God speaking to us about our lives? You might wait because you are hoping God will show you the next steps. I believe He does show you more when you wait with an expectant heart!

If you are a momma bear and daddy bear caring for those babies, God is talking to you too. You might be working on a big project and keep telling yourself, "When life slows down, I will spend time with God." Or your full-time job might be at a church. You think the time at work is the same as spending time with God. Every time the doors are open, you are signed up to serve. Doing for God can't take the place of what God has already done for you.

A friend and I were talking about this very subject. She was a fit to be tied; only you, Southern gals, are going to know what I am talking about. How about her panties were a bit in a wad. Do you get what I am trying to say now? Haha. She had experienced one too many times, someone else stealing her ideas. I guess they didn't steal them but took the ideas and acted on them. I get it; that feeling, someone is stealing from you.

I was working on this book and found books with "joy" in the title. My first response was, "Why, God!" I am writing that book, but then I had to remember I am not the only one called to write about joy. Joy must be a message God is wanting to get out in the world.

If you see someone taking your ideas, let it go. Remember that your story, your creation, your book, your business ideas will be different because of you. The flavor you bring will make it different. The bottom line is my friend was upset because she was tired of missing God. She was tired of feeling like God was taking her ideas away from her.

I ravish books. Reading books is my superpower. When I am flipping through books in a bookstore or scanning titles, I sometimes come across a word or quote, and I am scratching my head, thinking, *Now, why didn't I write my book sooner!* I have said it once, and I will say it again, life is too short for us to not take risks.

What fun is life if lived in your comfort zones?

What is the point in living if you are going to do the same thing over and over again? I do have some friends who will tell you they thrive on routine. The majority of you reading this will probably feel the same way. But what about the wild ones? The ones who are spontaneous and don't need a schedule. The ones who live to make up their own rules. I am talking to you.

GOT COURAGE

I am talking to the ones who wake up every day asking themselves, "What scary thing can I do today?" Have you seen that movie, "I Bought a Zoo"? One of my favorite parts is when the main character, Benjamin, played by Matt Damon, says, "You know, sometimes all you need is twenty seconds of insane courage. Just literally twenty seconds of just embarrassing bravery. And I promise you, something great will come of it." Boom! Now do I have your attention?

Who is following along with me now? I know life is hard, and some horrible things have happened in your life. I know you might be scared, but one of my favorite female preachers is Joyce Meyer. She taught me that you feel the fear and do it anyway! If you wait for the fear to pass, then you are going to be spending a lifetime of waiting. Or should I rephrase, you will waste a lifetime.

The other amazing thing I know is that God doesn't waste a thing. There isn't one thing that has happened in your life that He can't use for His glory. He loves you so much! He will take the most horrific crimes and abuse against you and bring purpose. He will bring glorious purpose out of your painful places, the hidden spaces in your mind and heart that you have tucked away. You might think they are locked away. You might have tossed the key and hope to never find it.

Those are the spaces that God knows about and wants to come in with His unconditional love and heal. I get it! You don't ever want to visit them. I am here to remind you; this journey doesn't have to be done alone. You are not alone; you have others who see you, know you, and understand. God loves you and is cheering you on.

We lose perspective, sometimes, when our focus is on what we don't have. Did you wake up today? Open your eyes and blink ten times. Pinch the side of your arm; did you feel that? You are alive, and God is not done with you yet. You are on an assignment and His special agent.

GOT AVAILABILITY

Now, don't you feel special, knowing that someone needs you? Someone out there needs you! How does that make you feel? I don't know who your someone is, but we need one another. God blesses His people by using people to be a blessing.

The Lord is calling you on a new mission. He has all the plans written out. The first question and business is: are you available? Will you be available to the things of God? Can He trust you with a new mission? The mission will probably be scary but remember what you have been praying for. Lord, use me. Again, it is alright if you feel afraid, "Feel the fear and do it anyway!" I have been there too, but our God is so serious about you! He wants to reveal your purpose to you. There is a world full of people who don't know Him. We are living in the midst of broken hearts in a hurting world. What part are you going to play in being an agent of change? Shall we look at what God's Word says?

"I, Paul, am under God's plan as an apostle, a special agent of Christ Jesus, writing to you faithful believers in Ephesus" (Ephesians 1:1, MSG).

Shall we insert our own name and replace Ephesus with United States or whatever country you are from? This is what I love about the word of God. It is up close and personal. Would you believe I found this verse the morning after staying up way too late and tirelessly typing? I knew I had something good to share, and I was grateful for the confirmation the next day that I was on the right track.

Most special agents are involved in an investigation of large-scale criminal activity. Does that sound like the world we live in? You turn on the TV and hear about someone getting busted for drugs. You hop on social media and see an article about a ring of sex traffickers caught. Young children, women, men, the elderly are being abused. Are you going to sit back and feel helpless? What are you going to be about it? How are you going to be a special agent and help someone? Too many times, we wait for someone else to do it when God is waiting on us to be that someone else.

Where is your part to play? How can you be a part of the solution and not whine about the problems? Oh, you better believe there is a cost to pay. If we are honest with ourselves, the cost is too high. We walk around life with one eye open and one eye closed. Just maybe, if we pretend it isn't happening, then it will go away. We won't have to move off of our comfy couches and give up our favorite night of TV shows.

You know why I can talk so boldly; I am no different than you. I will rephrase that statement. I used to be no better than you. When the Lord gets a hold of your heart, and you really embrace the reason you exist, your whole life changes!

Think about all of those swirling ideas, thoughts, and dreams that you have just been sitting on. God didn't waste any time in asking me why I was sitting on my hands. He was saying, "You are a special agent! I am not done with revealing your passions and purpose to you." He is saying the same to you!

When you are wide awake, you fantasize about being a super-hero. You want to be someone who is brave. You want to move out of your comfort zone. You want to go to bed at night with that full feeling that you made a difference in someone's life today. This is a friendly voice saying, "Just do something! Just do anything! Just put your feet to faith."

I know it feels like you might throw up. Throw up and keep

putting one foot forward at a time towards that thing that keeps haunting you. The deep calling you, do you hear that ringing noise in your ear to do more?

When I received my first copy of *Wild Joy* after being professionally edited, I felt like I was on a roller coaster! When reading the comments and editing this book one more time, I seriously felt all the feels, all the flutters in my belly were real, and it wasn't any baby fluttering! Ha.

The dreams you have, the ones that wake you up, the ones that you wake up in a cold sweat! Those dreams! You know those recurring dreams you just can't shake. God is nudging you closer and closer to your purpose.

My prayer is that you will not be the same after reading this book. You will take heed to the call. You will start moving towards your audacious dreams. More than likely, they are something you haven't even shared with your spouse or closest friends. You are scared to open your mouth because what if you fail. What if you don't fail? What if you experience the wild joy I am talking about? What if you tap into a ministry or career the Lord has been waiting for you to start? A joy that is only found outside of yourself. A purpose that is set aside for you to pursue.

I have two examples in my own life where I feel like I have made the most difference. The first one is the women's ministry, Beautiful Warriors. The year 2020 makes a decade I have been leading and serving amazing women. For the first eight years, we gathered in various places. My goal was fellowship! To include food, friendship, and freedom. The event wasn't complete without a good word. You could find a group of hungry women in bowling alleys, parks, restaurants, particularly Mexican establishments. I enjoyed hosting our annual pool party. As the year ended, I also couldn't wait for ooey-gooey toasted marshmallows on top of thin pieces of chocolate bar smashed between graham crackers. The bonfire events are a big hit!

I also was honored to go into a women's prison. My first visit was Mother's Day 2011. Who knew God would take my testimony and message of hope into a female correctional facility. I was afraid but more excited to go in places most people would never visit. I was so thankful to be on the outside of those bars. My greatest blessing was witnessing some women live in such a freedom, they didn't let the bars and barbed wire fences hold them hostage.

YOU ARE A SPECIAL AGENT

I guess you could say I had my own group of special agents. The Aglow ladies who I ministered in prison with are special agents. I was one of the youngest, and those beautiful, brave women could have been sitting at home. They choose to sacrifice their time for the hurting.

My mission amongst the fun and food with Beautiful Warriors was for women to feel empowered. They would leave feeling a bit braver after hearing other women's stories—the connections and support when life was hard. A sisterhood was being built. A multitude of women cheering one another to succeed. What if the world looked like this? If women and men would rise up and know their worth, we could solve half of the world's problems. I do believe we are fighting against evil.

"The thief only comes to steal and kill and destroy; I have come that they may have life and have it to the full" (John 10:10, NIV).

A few days before the summer of 2020, I had a dream that will forever change my life. This was not any ordinary dream. I was a spiritual assassin! I was on an assignment to break the neck of the enemy. My dream was full of twists and turns. I literally broke necks in my dream. Not just one time but three times. I woke up remembering the details. I was half asleep with one eye open jotting down key things.

I was very startled, too. It took me about forty-five minutes to go back to sleep. I knew this dream was very different. I am grateful for all Beautiful Warrior women who share my excitement for dreams as much as I do. I sent a couple of them messages with details because I needed some help on what the Lord was speaking to me. I didn't want to miss a thing! Not one single thing!

They helped me figure out what I was to learn in the assassin dream.

Who really knows what God is doing in your life! It reminds me of a Bible verse in the book of Daniel.

"He reveals deep and hidden things; he knows what lies in darkness, and light dwells with him" (Daniel 2:22, NIV).

This Bible verse also represents how God speaks to us in numbers. The earth, the world, is so full of signs and wonders. Have you slowed down enough to see them? I talked about my experiences with numbers in other chapters.

I can look back over my life and see times when God was there for me. I didn't see it at the time, but now I do see Jesus. I know it has taken years and years of healing. I will also add months and months of counseling before a flashlight could be shined down on the happy and good moments of my childhood. Those times I shared about blocking out the good and the bad memories. Where was the joy in those days? The joy was Jesus, who I accepted at eleven years old. He never ever left! Not in the sexual abuse, neglect, or abandonment!

He is not going to leave you either! He loves you and wants only the best for you. He is a good Father. The enemy is the one who tried to come against you as a small, powerless child. He didn't try, He did! Those attacks look different for all of us.

Let's not lose sight of our creator and maker, who loves you beyond your understanding. God didn't want any of those horrible things to happen to you. You can fill in the blank with the "things." Your story might not involve rape, adultery, divorce, abuse, suicide, addictions, and lots of loss. I am so sorry for the pain others inflicted on you. Many times, what happened to you wasn't your fault! I know it is hard to understand why God let horrible things happen to you. That lingering question, why do bad things happen to good people?

If I am not careful, I can allow my mind to get stuck in dark places. I am not the scared, helpless, and insecure little girl anymore! I am a warrior who knows why God made her and is loved beyond her comprehension. As I share parts of my life, I want you to think about your own. The whole purpose of me writing my book is for you to tap into your joy moments.

I was reading a book about stinking thinking. It was a birthday gift; I felt obligated to read it. Haha. As it sat on my dresser, I passed by it several times, and something kept me from picking it up. As I was reading the pages, facts about stress were stated. Would you believe that 70 percent of our thoughts are negative? We stress over work, finances, relationships, etc. So, only 30 percent of our thoughts are of joy, hope, peace, and love.

It was such a reminder to me that I had to finish my *Wild Joy* book. I was like, "Lord, I hear You!" Most people do not experience joy, and I have been given a mission of helping others explore joy in their lives. I not only want to help you explore, but I want you to find joy. This is a treasure hunt. The treasure is the joy found in the wilderness. What brings your life joy? Are you capturing the simple moments of joy?

Back to my spiritual assassin dream, it wasn't about joy but about a mission. God spoke to me about what He wanted me to do. He showed me where the darkness was coming from. He showed me new strategy of how to take the enemy out. He gave me the strength to break the neck of the enemy. Yes, me! So wild thinking about it.

When I obey my mission in real life, you know what I find? Yes, you got it—joy. Joy, joy, unspeakable joy. The Lord gave me a warning in my dream. He was showing me people aren't always who we think they are. Some people might be wearing a mask, so their true identity isn't revealed. If your heart is to really know the truth, then God will show you. It might not happen in your dreams like mine. It might be delivered through people, someone on the street, or someone close to you. It might be in a book, a song, or a vision. I don't know how God speaks to you.

Again, dear friends, if you think I am speaking a foreign language, then welcome to a new way of life. I introduced you to God's way of living. The verse in John comes alive over and over again. Jesus came to give life and give it in abundance. If you are living in survival mode, I am yelling at the rooftops for you to experience the zoe life that is available to you. The zoe life is full of love, joy, peace, and abundance.

Are you a warrior? A warrior is one who fights! A warrior is someone who fights for others. A warrior is someone who doesn't quit; you stay in the battle. It isn't about getting knocked down but about how many times you get back up and the strength you grow in the process. This strength isn't always from within but from God. Or do you fit more in the category of a worrier? Someone who worries all the time. Someone who doesn't trust God but thinks they know best. There is no judgment, just an invitation to exchange the worrier for the warrior. I am offering an invitation to become more, to step into your mission of a special agent.

CHAPTER 17:
Finishing Touches

Keep your eyes on Jesus, who both began and finished this race we're in.

Hebrews 12:2 (MSG)

The Merriam-Webster dictionary defines finish like this: something that completes or perfects.

Jesus is our perfector. I have good news for you. You do not have to go through life trying to be perfect anymore. Perfect is only one man, and His name is Jesus. You were not born to live a life of perfection. You were born in the image of Jesus. The acts of perfect living will only leave you worn out—spinning your wheels in the cycle of trying. Trying and not ever really getting anywhere or accomplishing what you were created to do! You try, try, and try some more but only find yourself feeling deflated and defeated.

I know this to be true because I have lived it. These aren't just words flippantly coming out of my mouth and onto this page. I tried to share mistakes I made and personal stories to remind you of that one simple but *big* thing—*you* are not alone!

You might not have been able to relate to a mother who committed suicide or a dad who was absent and caused you to question his love. You might not have related to losing your dad so unexpectedly or even growing up with a father. You might have parents who raised you well and weren't able to relate to me talking about my parents who struggled with their addictions. You might have never been married, experienced divorce or loser boyfriends.

I am sure most of us have, at some point, went through relationships that were not healthy or right for us. You might not be a mom or a wife or husband or dad but what I do know is you are a child of God.

Jesus was thinking of you when he took his final breath.

This one act is a perfect example of unconditional love. A reminder of God's nature, His

character, and adoration for you. I need to hear over and over again how much God loves me. It drove me to share about His love from beginning to end in *Wild Joy.* God loves *you!* My prayer and heart cry is for you to see it, you feel it, you believe it, and you receive it. Some words need to be declared and repeated again and again for you to start living it out. Can you imagine what your life would be like if you lived from a place of "I am loved"?

YOU ARE LOVED

You are loved! I am loved! You are loved!

Even after all my words and stories, if you still feel distant from Jesus, if you are still

questioning, wondering, and seeking why then let me reassure you, Jesus sees you. He meets you exactly where you are. You might not be seeking Him, but I can promise you, He is seeking you!

As I finished up this last chapter, I was going through a very hard season of my life. I thought the loss of my dad and the loss of my mom were tough, but, my awesome readers, this season was a new kind of tough that I was experiencing. A tough that will leave your eyes swollen and puffy from all the tears.

The loss of my beautiful sweet mother-in-law, Joyce, many know her as Granny. The days of who she used to be were quickly fading away. The loss of road trips, goodwill visits, yard sales, ice cream stops, and watching HGTV. The loss of her mental health. The loss of conversations when I knew what she was saying before the long-suffering days of dementia. The loss of being able to care for her full-time. The loss of this angelic woman residing in my home. The loss of being able to see her first thing in the morning and tuck her in at night. The loss of one more mother. So much loss but so much joy and beauty intertwined.

As you have gotten to know me a bit better, I hope you feel like we are friends. If you saw me in the bookstore, at the beach, or in a grocery store shopping the produce aisle, I hope you would wave, give me a high five, or yell my name. You and I have a lot in common, our stories are different, and our pain is different but our goal to finish well and reach the finish line is the same.

I wrote this poem in that tough season, a time of loss and sorrow. I had no idea what the next few months would hold. I didn't know what the next steps were in Joyce's well-being. I remembered thinking about the scary days ahead. I didn't have a plan, but I knew the one I could call on who did, Jesus.

Your Plan

Your time, not mine.

Granny will go be with you

When you say so not I

Your plan, not mine

One minute, one day

One week, one month

You say when not I

To see Granny go

To watch her slip away

One minute, one day

Your plan, not mine.

You love, Granny

Not a question in my mind

I feel your peace

Even in this place

Time doesn't seem kind

But your love never wastes away

Joannie Garner

I thought we were going to lose her this day. It seemed she would cross over but as my words in the above poem state, not my plan but God's plan. In times when you are uncertain about the days to come. Please be comforted in the peace of God. There were many decisions to be made. I felt the heavy weight of making the right choice. To be honest, it felt like a no-win for everyone. I was not confident in which direction I would go. I did know I felt these words, "I *did not* ask for *this*!"

What, in your own life, feels like rough waters that you are navigating and saying, "I did not ask for this"?

Can I just be real with you; you are so very right. You did not ask for this. Life has a way of bringing opportunities that make you want to go outside and scream at the top of your lungs. Okay, maybe this is just my "extra" friends. The rest of you are okay with hitting your pillow.

Seriously, I don't know your story but can only offer you my stories.

I did continue to listen for the voice of God concerning Joyce. We would eventually be led to release Joyce into full-time health care. God was on the scene! He provided one next step at a time which way to go concerning my mother-in-law. It was so very hard to let her go, to give someone else full access to care of her life. Once again, trust was my focus. To trust God's great plan, not my own.

I was really surprised when God started asking me, what do you want Joannie concerning Joyce. That question, what do you want? I didn't know…it took some deep thinking to answer it. When I got honest, I wanted to feel free, I wanted to be able to make lunch plans, go on spontaneous trips, and not have to worry about if something was going to happen to my mother-in-law.

I wanted the best care for Joyce. I knew deep down I was not the one to give her the mental and physical care she needed. I had to release her. I had to trust God had her and love her way more than me. He was going to protect her and make sure she was taken care. I want to encourage you if you are caring for a loved one. God sees you and is asking you the same question. "What do you want?" Do you know? Can you answer him honestly?

YOU ARE FORGIVEN

I also want to highlight the one who forgives! He forgave you so we could forgive others. I want to share a story with you about my dad. I thought this would be the perfect spot to tell it. I had a hard time over the years in forgiving my dad. It wasn't easy for me because I lived most of my life justifying his actions. I knew only parts of how my dad was raised. His siblings shared some stories about their childhood that brought me to tears. My grandfather was a man who battled with his own demons. He struggled with abusing alcohol and the ones he loved. A sad story, he ended walking away from his family, which meant the oldest siblings were left to

pick up the pieces and lead their family. My dad was the oldest son, and I know he had to grow up too fast.

"Be kind and compassionate to one another, forgiving each other, just as in Christ God forgave you" (Ephesians 4:32, NIV).

As you know, he passed away before reading this book. His story isn't mine to tell, but parts of his story are mine because I am his daughter. He left a legacy in his children.

The best honor I know how to give my dad is to live my life for Jesus! I still have my days when I struggle. I still say and do things that aren't so nice. I still have a bit of a temper; we are all a working progress, right! Over the years, Jesus taught me how to forgive my dad. He showed me a visual of a cross and asked me if I was worthy of being nailed to that cross. Of course, my answer was no. Who am I to be on the cross like Jesus? Who was I to not forgive my dad when my heavenly Father sent His only Son to forgive me of my sins? I am forgiven, and so are you!

Jesus forgives! You are forgiven! He died on the cross for your sins and mine so we could live a life of freedom.

God started showing me the unforgiveness that was still lingering in my heart. I still had places that needed healing. My dad was an amazing man but battled with his own trauma and unhealed wounds. He lived to see three women he loved die. One was my mom and her suicide. The other was a tragic car accident. The fifth wife and his last wife died of a drug overdose

. My dad knew loss, but I am sure he didn't know how to grieve. I think that is why he struggled with his addictions. How does one get through all those deaths without Jesus? I have no clue! Talk about survivor's guilt! I told you he loved women; he might have had more out there. LOL. I am scared to do the blood test everyone is doing; I might find some new siblings.

If you don't already feel like you know Jesus, let me introduce you to Him again. I shared Jesus as a friend, lover, provider, protector, etc.

I want to end this book with Jesus, the finisher.

THE FINISHER

I will never forget this supernatural Tuesday that involved a day date with my husband. I might have been guilty of bribing him with food after. My man loves a good meal. I think I shared he is a quality time guy. I can usually win him over when food is involved, especially if it is just him and I. I love how my guy is into his wife, me, Mrs. Garner. He will pick me every time, and I feel so loved by him.

Friends, your heavenly Father, feels the same about you!

He will pick you every time!

The question is, do you pick *Him*?

Back to my story with my husband. He didn't know what to expect, but he trusted me when I asked him to go on the day date.

Is Jesus asking you on a day date? Is he asking you to go on a wild joy journey with Him? Has Jesus been asking you to go, and you have been too afraid to go?

Now, let me say, Tim did know that our day date would involve church. I didn't want him to feel tricked; no one likes a bait and switch, right? I knew once he experienced the atmosphere, he would understand what the big deal was all about, why I came home so full of God's winks and excitement about basking in the presence of Jesus.

Can I just say, I have been to many different churches and experienced a lot of denominations over the years? This was not your ordinary everyday church. This was church like you see in those shoot-'em-up movies. Ha, the ones where the good guys are hiding out from the bad guys, thinking they are safe. But the bad guys don't care if you are in a church. They come in with blazing guns, ready or not.

This church I am describing was so much better than any movie. We all know movies are staged and not real life. This was real life. Can you see why I couldn't wait for my husband to

experience the glory I had the past couple of months? I was floating on cloud Jesus! Y'all, can you picture with me a little hideaway? Turn with me to Psalm 27. Check out the NIV translation.

"One thing I ask from the Lord, this only do I seek: that I may dwell in the house of the Lord all the days of my life, to gaze on the beauty of the Lord and to seek him in his temple" (Psalm 27:4, NIV).

Is it okay to ask where His temple is in your life? Where do you gaze? Is your life full of beauty? Some questions to ponder on and ask yourself over the next few weeks. We have been on a journey of wild joy together. It has been a wild ride, and I do believe your best days are ahead of you.

Seek: to resort, to go in search of, look for, to try to discover, to ask for.

I was seeking the Lord; I was looking for a place to heal my broken heart after my dad's death. I found the perfect safety net to allow my heart to heal. I have experienced many losses but nothing like the one of losing my father.

God's Word brought healing, hope, and happiness.

"I'm asking God for one thing, only one thing: To live with him in his house my whole life long. I'll contemplate his beauty; I'll study at his feet" (Psalm 27:4, MSG).

This part really gets me, got me in that season, and still gets me!

"That's the only quiet, secure place in a noisy world. The perfect getaway, far from the buzz of traffic" (Psalm 27:5, MSG).

Again, where do you go to get away? I shared many of my favorite places, but none can compare to the presence of Jesus. As I stated before, your quiet place, your time with God, isn't always a place of no noise or away from everyone. Sometimes the best you can do is get away in your vehicle on the way to work, grocery store, gas station, or a friend's house.

WHITE SPACES

I have even been known to sit in my vehicle for a few minutes to gather my thoughts. I have a dear friend who is like my sister, who just recently got married and said to me the other day, "I know what you mean now about taking time to sit in your vehicle." I said, "Yep, the white spaces of my day. It is so important to take time for yourself. To take those few minutes before you enter back in with your family."

I have a cool story to share from 2021 about this cool getaway church I am describing that could be found in an action-packed movie.

My daughter came with me to CTK one very rainy Tuesday. She and I sat in the left-hand corner, closer to the back than the front. Something about that back row Baptist thing, I guess. We were standing up to get ready for prayer and communion. It was a serene time while the bishop took his communion and prepared it for others.

Josie leaned close to me and said, "Mom, I don't like the silence." I said, "Sweetie, there are so many gifts in the silence." Then I just nudged her a bit; a sweet, momma nudge with my shoulder. It felt like time stopped. It was a moment of white space. A time when the worldly clocks stopped for God to breathe into the sacred space. For activity to cease and eyes closed, to stop and really soak up the moment.

Can we say this was the year no one will ever forget? The year of quarantine! The year when life would change as we knew it. The year when it wasn't strange to see people wearing masks, face shields, and handkerchiefs over their face! The year that would define history! I remember the big hype and scare around 2000, but it doesn't even hold a candle to 2020!

Many places were closing. The only way you could attend church services was online. Did you ever think churches would close in all parts of the world? This was a pandemic like never before! Who thought that Sunday mornings would be spent at home. No more church building to share a time of worship and fellowship. This little sanctuary I found was a place of solace, protection, and hope from all the outside fear and noise.

Fear swept over America, and most people didn't know how to protect themselves or deal with the spread of COVID. In my time at this church, my heart was comforted, and I felt at home. My heart was able to feel peace like never before! This might sound silly, but the atmosphere smelled of heaven. I know, I know, how do I know what heaven smells like? Ha! I don't, but I could only imagine. A sweet fragrance of God's love permeating.

It also helped that the people were so kind and inviting. It only took a short time to not feel like an outsider. To be honest, I didn't even care! I only wanted to come, sit, and receive. I really didn't even have the mental energy for conversations. I was hoping I could sneak in and sneak out. Have you ever been there, where you just wanted to blend in and not be noticed?

Who doesn't love a lunchtime surprise? These church services were called noonday, an hour service, giving up your lunch hour. Speaking of lunch, I told you I promised Tim a nice lunch after the service. He just needed to endure the hour. I forgot to mention I also reminded him to be on his best behavior. You will see why this was important as I continue to share. Just hold on a bit longer, I know I am dragging this out, but it will be worth it! The small details matter, right!

Tim and I sat down in the pews a few mins before church service started. This allowed him time to check out his surroundings. Most military men want to scan the room before they feel comfortable. They also don't like to sit with their backs to anyone. That was hard not to do, but we sat in the back. I was not used to my guy being a bit distracted, but we couldn't help his back to the door. I was a-okay as he looked behind him every few seconds.

Who remembers the saying, back row Baptist? This Friday, Tim and I were; as we sat in the back of the church. I was okay with that, too, because my heart was so happy to have my husband sitting beside me in this beautiful place. One of the first things Tim saw was this word, *Tetelestai.*

TETELESTAI

This word was carved in the center of the wooden table in the front of the church. It was in the center of the room where you could not miss it. My husband's eyes were drawn right to it! It was near the beautiful display with the communion table. My eyes and imagination went straight to the wine goblets. I thought back to the days of Jesus, when He was a man walking on earth.

Can you imagine meeting Him then, seeing Him as a small boy preaching to the multitudes? It is hard for me not to compare my mom's age and the age of Jesus when He started His ministry; they were both thirty years old! My mom only lived thirty years on this earth, and Jesus was the same age, who left behind everything as He knew it to minister to the lost, the demon-possessed, and the brokenhearted.

One of the first things I noticed was the way the clergymen were dressed. They had on white robes. Some of them had a sash over their neck that hung down over their shirt. The other thing that captured my eye and attention was the paintings covered from wall to wall. The fine intricate details in the canvases depicted a story of the life of Jesus.

I was stopped in time by the events that led up to the crucifixion of Jesus. One also couldn't miss the beautiful tapestry that hung in the front of the church. My eyes darted to and fro from the stained glass windows, wooden crosses, swords, and remembrance of Jesus. I was seeing some very symbolic presentations of life in the early Christian days.

The communion was prepared for all to see it; the words spoke leading up to it were

unforgettable. The whole experience was a piece of wild joy. My husband immediately was

drawn to that word carved in the pew. We both looked at each other, bewildered as to what *tetelestai* meant; neither of us knew.

Tim leaned over to tell me he found it! Tetelestai meant it is finished. Tetelestai comes from the verb *teleo*, which means "to bring an end, to complete, to accomplish."

We both felt a holy hush. If you are ever in the Selma, Alabama area, stop in, I know they would love to have you! Google, Cathedral of Christ the King, and your GPS will take you right there. Tell me Joannie sent you. Wink wink.

We were in the presence of the I Am! The Alpha and the Omega, the beginning and the end. Please join me, gather your Bible and turn to the book of John. What a way to finish *Wild Joy*, reading my favorite book of the Bible. As you read, picture with me, the last words to leave the lips of Jesus. These were the last words that Jesus spoke

> *"When he had received the drink, Jesus said, 'It is finished.' With that, he bowed his head and gave up his spirit" (John 19:20, NIV).*

> *"It is finished" (John 19:30, NIV).*

Afterword

The memory on Facebook helped guide me to the completion of *Wild Joy*. I saw the memory and picture of Josie and me, lying on my bed, working on this manuscript. I could not believe it was exactly one year to the day of signing the contract with Trilogy Publishing. What if I wouldn't have started! What if my intentions were good, but I never set aside time each day to write? You would not be reading *Wild Joy*. I was blown away but knew it was another God wink.

The end of January 2021 was when God started speaking to me about fasting. In this

season of spiritual fasting, I would start to not only clean up my life but also my physical body. I asked God to help me detox things to include food, habits, people, and places that were no longer serving my life well. I knew He wanted to take me places I had never been, and I had to ask myself if I was willing to do things I had never done. I had to be willing to exchange the old things for the new He was offering me.

The book cover was inspired by the amazing joy adventure of Josie and I parasailing. I knew I wanted my cover to be bright and full of color. Joy has brought so much color and light to my life. As I sat on the edge of the boat, I realized I needed help to go up. I couldn't parasail on my own. I had to trust others to take me where I couldn't go on my own. I had to trust the process. This whole publishing process has felt the same way. I was not going to be able to alone take *Wild Joy* to the places God wanted it to go. I had to ask for help and trust others to help me take this book to those wild, weird, and wonderful spaces.

I was praying, fasting, and asking God to bring people and resources to complete the

birthing of *Wild Joy*. In that season, I came across this verse that embodies what I was feeling and didn't fully have words to

241

communicate.

> *That's why I don't think there's any comparison between the present hard times and the coming good times. The created world itself can hardly wait for what's coming next. Everything in creation is being more or less held back. God reins it in it until both creation and all the creatures are ready and can be released at the same moment into the glorious times ahead. Meanwhile, the joyful anticipation deepens. All around us we observe a pregnant creation. The difficult times of pain throughout the world are simply birth pangs. But it's not only around us; it's within us. The Spirit of God is arousing us within. We're also feeling the birth pangs. These sterile and barren bodies of ours are yearning for full deliverance. That is why waiting does not diminish us, any more than waiting diminishes a pregnant mother. We are enlarged in the waiting. We, of course, don't see what is enlarging us. But the longer we wait, the larger we become, and the more joyful our expectancy.*

Romans 8:18-25 (MSG)

I felt like I was in the birthing room, pushing and more pushing, waiting for the birth of *Wild Joy*. God always confirms what He is doing with His Word. Again, are you paying attention? Are you listening to the voice of God? I found this verse the week of signing the contract. God knew I would need truth to combat any lies or doubt I was feeling.

I also had a cool revelation about six months after my dad passed about Jesus and my dad

talking about a big project that would distract me from my dad's death. The loss of my dad was one of the hardest losses I have ever experienced. I had to find joy and humor in the special conversation where the meeting took place for God to whisper the vision of *Wild Joy*. The vision between my earthly father and heavenly Father brought peace, love, and comfort. It helped balance the days of doubt, fear, and questioning, "Do I have what it takes?" I got through because I knew this project was much bigger than myself.

None of this fazes us because Jesus loves us. I'm absolutely convinced that nothing—nothing living or dead, angelic or demonic, today or tomorrow, high or low, thinkable or unthinkable—absolutely nothing can get between us and God's love because of the way that Jesus our Master has embraced us.

Romans 8:37-39 (MSG)

Good ole Facebook did it again. I saw a memory from May 2017 that reminded me I was

in the right place at the right time. I posted pictures wearing hot pink boxing gloves. I was at a local TBN station in Montgomery being interviewed about staying in the fight for women. I felt so loved by God, knowing I was walking in the plans He had for me. I want to leave you with a few thoughts and practical steps as you continue to move forward. The key to getting anywhere in life is putting one foot forward at a time.

I am thanking you from the bottom of my heart for taking a chance on this first-time author. I appreciate you and your support in buying my book, *Wild Joy*.

Lasting Thoughts

Read the Bible. Psalms and Proverbs in conjunction with the day of the week.

Keep a journal near; God is always speaking.

Heart check, end of the day.

Being nice to others doesn't mean you disrespect yourself.

Give yourself grace in the space.

Feel the fear and do it anyway.

God doesn't want you to get over it. He wants you to go through it.

Sunshine always does a body and mind good!

A smile doesn't cost you much. Tell your face you are happy.

Joy is a journey; you don't get there overnight.

God is wildly in love with you!

To you, my wild joy seekers:

Thank you for taking the time to read *Wild Joy*.

I appreciate you joining me on my journey. I am praying that God reveals the wild, weird and wonderful spaces in your own journey.

I also pray that you encounter a real relationship with Jesus full of His unconditional love, not just rules and religion.

I pray you discover your purpose, the purpose only you can accomplish on this earth. God is calling you to an adventure and partnership in pursuing your dreams.

I also pray you allow God to heal those broken pieces because He wants to make a beautiful mosaic out of the messes in your life.

Your story is still being written, and the Lord is sending a message to the world with your name attached to it.

With deep joy and gratitude,

Your friend,

Joannie.

Endnotes

[1] www.5lovelanguages.com

[2] www.meriam-webster.com

[3] www.chistianity.com

CPSIA information can be obtained
at www.ICGtesting.com
Printed in the USA
LVHW082126261021
701302LV00008B/7

9 781637 696569